# Which Way To Starboard?

## Memoir of a Lifelong Sailor and Wooden Boat Enthusiast

## Guy G. Lemieux

iUniverse, Inc.
Bloomington

## Which Way To Starboard?
## Memoir of a Lifelong Sailor and Wooden Boat Enthusiast

iUniverse books may be ordered through booksellers or by contacting:

iUniverse
1663 Liberty Drive
Bloomington, IN 47403
www.iuniverse.com
1-800-Authors (1-800-288-4677)

ISBN: 978-1-4502-8089-1 (pbk)
ISBN: 978-1-4502-8090-7 (ebk)

Printed in the United States of America

iUniverse rev. date: 3/7/11

# Preface

From a very young age a boy is taunted by his fathers dream to sail. Only after his marriage does he get his first taste of a water vessel and his first sail trial. It would be another eighteen years before he would really get his feet wet. From there on there was no stopping him. He was faced with all kinds of challenges from the fear of drowning to the excitement of racing.

It leads him into the purchasing and renovating of a wooden boat, a long drawn out affair which leaves him discourage on many occasions. With a profound devotion, he dusts himself off and continues on his journey. The author certainly lives his life to the fullest around boats. The wind and water becomes his freedom. To him all boats are beautiful, fun to watch, and to play with. He never abandoned his dream and even implied his children into sailing, to a point of helping them buy a sailboat. There was no end to his interests in boats and water, forever dreaming of new adventures.

The author gives a firsthand account about the sport of family sailing and being around boats. Either the reader becomes initiated into the sport of sailing or through his own evaluations, he backs off.

# Acknowledgements

Special thanks to all my loved ones and others who helped me to nurture my dream and allowed me to confide in them. Without their participation in one way or another, I might not have lived my dream.

Thank you to my sister, Lise Snyder, for believing in my book and spending all those hours correcting my drafts. I could never say enough thank-you's.

A special thank you to my editor, Angela Bellacosa, for doing such a fine job editing my book in a most agreeable and professional manner. Mme. Bellacosa is very talented in her work.

What I lived and shared with my children during these moments will forever be in our hearts. Throughout our lives, there's never a wrong time for doing something; it is always the right time. We learned to work and play together, to laugh and squeal and run and jump and … sail.

Thank you, to my three children,
Roxanne, Francois, and Marc

# Table of Contents

# 1. So Close, So Far

My father, two of my uncles, and my grandfather, who was in the Merchant Navy during WWII, had all worked on boats on the Great Lakes. Needless to say, the love of water runs in my blood.

One early summer day in Welland Ontario, back in 1954, my father took the family out for a car ride. At ten years old, I found this kind of thing boring. I would have preferred to stay at home. My father being a dreamer had a way of promising us dreams that never materialized – or more precisely, dreams that were unattainable. On this occasion, we drove to a quaint little place on the Niagara Peninsula called Port Dalhousie. We walked through this luscious park of tall, wide trees that spread their cool shade everywhere. Upon approaching a galvanized fence near the water's edge, we stopped and gazed at a mooring site with tiny sailboats all lazily floating, tied to their buoys. In the mirror-like water appeared their reflections, which doubled the number of sailboats. I was barely able to reach high enough to peek over the fence, and having to look through it was annoying. My father had a better view of this mystic haven of sailing crafts suspended in time.

It was here that my father described what it felt like to control a sailboat with your fingertips, and how a sailboat displaced itself quietly and effortlessly through the water. I interrupted to say, "The cabins look small on them, Dad!" He told us that the cabins were only there for an overnight sleep or when the sailors got caught in a downpour. The sailboats I was so fascinated by that day were really very small boats, smaller than what I had expected. They were twenty to twenty five feet long and had beams of seven feet at the very most. They appeared low and sleek on the water. They were all made of wood and painted white, red, dark green, or navy

1

blue, with a narrow white or red boot stripe at water level. They looked delightful, almost toyish, these little sailing vessels. They all had sparkling, varnished splashboards leading aft from each side of the cabin; these helped to keep the cockpit dry when sailing in choppy waters. The cabin tops were all painted or smartly varnished, and had small, round or oval, brass portholes on each side. They had a sliding hatch with cross boards to block the companionway from intruders such as flies, mosquitoes, and the rain.

"Dad, how do these people get to and from their boats?"

My father answered, "They all have a dingy for that; a small rowboat used to transport them, their lunches, and other belongings, including their sailing partner or partners."

He explained to us that these toys were exactly that. "They're to play with in the wind and water. Only you sit on them and harness the wind with their sails, for they are the boat's motor."

"Dad, can the wind take you anywhere, in any direction, even at night?"

"That's just about right," my father answered.

That day was to be my first lesson of many in sailboats and sailing.

I had learned a poem at school, (in the fifth grade) earlier that year, and although I hated poems, I liked this one. I have always carried this poem in my heart.

## The Ships of Yule

When I was just a little boy,
Before I went to school,
I had a fleet of forty sail
I called the Ships of Yule;

Of every rig, from rakish brig
And gallant barkentine,
To little Fundy fishing boats
With gunwales painted green.

They used to go on trading trips
Around the world for me,
For though I had to stay on shore
My heart was on the sea.

They stopped at every port to call
From Babylon to Rome,
To load with all the lovely things
We never had at home;

With elephants and ivory
Bought from the King of Tyre,
And shells and silks and sandal-wood
That sailor men admire;

With figs and dates from Samarkand,
And squatty ginger-jars,
And scented silver amulets
From Indian bazaars;

With sugar-cane from Port of Spain,
And monkeys from Ceylon,
And paper lanterns from Pekin
With painted dragons on;

With cocoanuts from Zanzibar,
And pines from Singapore;
And when they had unloaded these
They could go back for more.

And even after I was big
And had to go to school,
My mind was often far away
Aboard the Ships of Yule.

~ William Bliss Carman

On another occasion, my father took me to a place on Lake Erie called Port Colborne. There was this little marina along the lakeshore just outside of town, (Ray's Livery), that had rowboats to rent along with a few motorized ones. They were used mostly for fishing. Not once did my father rent one, not even to take me out onto the water with. My heart and eyes were begging him in silence to do so, but to no avail. He never realized that I just wanted to go on a row boat, on any boat, even a raft if need be, just to float about on the water, to be detached from land. I knew we could not afford a sailboat. After a number of years, we were still at the same point, just helpless dreamers, tempted and filled with false hopes!

One weekend, my father took me on a trip to Port Dover, Ontario. Here I saw a different kind of boat, a small and tubby commercial fishing boat with high sides. It was completely enclosed to keep out the bad weather. These fishing boats, ugly as they were, intrigued me because of their gracefulness and agility, owing to their stout elephant shape, which indicated otherwise. That same day, surprisingly, my father lent me his precious fishing rod to pacify me. All that really mattered that day was that I was near water.

One holiday my family took me down east to Squatec, Quebec to visit my aunt and uncle on their farm. There was a boy my age, (a cousin), on this farm, and we became good friends. He invited me to go see the river behind their farm. Once there I noticed this raft that he had built. I was quick to get on it and we both began to play and then pole down the river. The raft was partially submerged because we were too heavy for it, but that didn't matter. We learned to keep our balance on it. We must have played for hours on this craft. It was exciting, floating away from land, floating down the river. At the end of the afternoon we tied the raft up to a tree and walked back to the farm. Time continued on for quite a while before something new entered my life.

From eleven to seventeen, I was at the public pool every day of the summer with my friends, and so I became an excellent swimmer. We would be tanning and swimming, swimming and tanning. What else could we do in the summertime? We swam in a pool that was right next to the Welland Canal, through which large cargo boats passed every day. Once, I even saw the Queen's yacht pass by. I believe it was called the *Britannia*. When I first saw it, I thought it looked like a cargo ship. I thought it should be smaller and more luxurious.

In 1961, at the age of seventeen, I joined the Canadian Navy. I wanted to leave home. There were bad vibes between my dad and me. It all stemmed from my being an adolescent – nothing major. I was proud and happy to be a Canadian Mariner. It was my first step towards attaining my goal, being around boats. At that time, anything seemed better than staying at home.

Invitation Bombardier and her master.

Invitation and the boys.

# 2. My First Sail

In 1965, I took my first summer vacation as a family man. My first wife and I went with her family to a place called Mary Lake, just outside the small town of Huntsville, Ontario. My father-in-law and his sister each had been given a cottage by their parents. There were five cottages that the grandparents had rented out for the last twenty years. It was such a gorgeous place to spend their summer vacations with their granddaughters, one of whom I had married.

There wasn't much interest on the part of my wife and in-laws in the nearby town of Huntsville, but what beautiful countryside. I was more or less freed from the stresses of the world outside during those two weeks. The repose helped me to release the accumulated tension inside of me, the excess stress caused by my job as a production foreman in a large rubber plant.

I was only 21 at the time, and I was in charge of the shipping department, which had eight loading docks and employed five dock workers. We loaded five to ten semis full of goods every day that were bound for Quebec, Ontario, and the Ford Motor Company in the US. Included were shipments to General Motors in Oshawa and The Chrysler Corporation in Windsor. It had taken me eight months to learn this job. I think this is the most difficult task that I have ever done. When my day was over, so was my mind. On top of this, I was in charge of two other departments totaling 55 workers. There were approximately 300-500 men and women employed there.

As I got up on the first morning at Mary Lake, there was a fair wind heading into the bay directly towards us. I liked the one-foot waves, which were accompanied by the odd white caps here and there. There was an island approximately a mile out, and interestingly enough, my in-laws had an old rowboat at the dock. I decided I needed some exercise, and I jumped into the boat, untied the lines, and ventured out. Oh, but it was easy and fun! The little swells grew a bit more in size as I passed Dilts Point. Then I found that the small challenge I had taken on had grown harder than what I had imagined.

I was preparing to turn around when suddenly I took on some water from the waves that were now hitting the boat across one side of the bow. I realized that turning around was not a good idea, so I turned back to my original heading and continued to row towards the island. To make headway I had to row very hard, and by now my hands had started to blister. *Only a little more,* I told myself, but it was almost unbearable. I wrapped my hands in my tee shirt, so I would be able to continue rowing. As I rowed towards the island for shelter, the waves became less menacing. Once there, I turned around and started on my way back. What a relief! Even though my hands continued to hurt and burn, I had an easier time returning. I just had to keep the boat straight with the odd row as the wind pushed me in. When I reached the dock, I was happy to be back. I had learned a valuable lesson, and that was never to take the weather for granted. It held its surprises, and it demanded respect. This was my first bout with the wind and water and their secrets.

I had married at twenty, with a baby on the way. I guess I had made all the right mistakes. I was at a loss what to do with myself. I thank my father in-law, for he came to the rescue. He had bought a clear varnished, cedar strip runabout, a beautiful little gem. With this, he gave me an adrenalin shot. This little beauty gave us a chance to water ski, tour the lake, and so forth. It was equipped with a 25 hp motor. He also had bought a 10 hp motor for the rowboat, which I used abundantly to go fishing.

On one of my fishing excursions, I had the 10 hp going full tilt as I was heading up the river from Mary Lake. The front end of the boat started sticking way up out of the water. The motor wasn't strong enough to push the boat out of the displacement stage to a planing one. I moved as far as I could toward the front of the boat, and suddenly the boat picked up speed as it flattened out. Wow, now I was hydroplaning. I didn't know that a flat bottom boat with an almost square sided chine was actually dangerous at high speeds compared to a v-bottom. When I began to turn, I thought it would be a normal maneuver, but to my surprise, I was almost thrown overboard because of the boat's quick reaction. The chine acted like a curved keel and the boat turned much faster than I had anticipated. I was lucky the boat didn't flip over. What a heart pounding experience. There was another lesson here: never overpower your boat!

The next day, not far from the dock, there was this young neighbor boy, maybe twelve years old, sailing some kind of box type boat, which I later found out was an Optimist Class daysailer. I walked over to see it, and was impressed by the fact that such a structure could sail. I asked the young lad if I could borrow his little sailing dingy to try it out, and he politely answered me no. Strict rule from his dad, but he could take me out on a sail if I liked. Now this I could not resist, and so we went out for a sail.

The daysailer didn't move any faster than I could swim. We were too heavy. Nonetheless, just seeing how it maneuvered in the wind, with the rocking and tugging it was so adventurous. I had my baptism, and it rekindled a childhood dream I had from the time I had gone to Port Dalhousie with my father. It was enough to get me fired up, and I started to buy the odd book on boats and sailing.

# 3. First Sailboat

Six years later, in 1971, my wife and I separated and divorced. I moved to Hamilton, which is on Lake Ontario. I made the acquaintance of a girl from my tennis club. I'd offered to take her out for a motorcycle ride, so one day we drove around until we pulled up to a stop just in front of Hamilton Harbour. I parked my motorcycle and we wandered over to a park bench and sat down. With my arm around her, I gave her a little squeeze as we gazed at a forty foot cement sailboat. It looked lonely under the moonlit sky. I mentioned to her that I'd always had this fantasy of making love on a sailboat during a moonlit night. I always thought that it would be so exciting and romantic. We huddled up even more. I harbored so many dreams in my heart. Would they ever come to life?

Later on that year I moved to Montréal to pursue life in whatever direction it would take me. Quite some time passed before the fall of 1972, when I had the chance to have a new girlfriend, my future wife, Jacinthe. She was a cute little nurse with blonde hair, blue eyes, and very bubbly. I remember on one occasion talking to her about how I hoped to build a sailboat someday, maybe just behind her parent's old shack of a cottage. They had another cottage right next door on the same property. I told her about my far-fetched ambition. I've always had this nagging desire to own a sailboat, to sail, and to travel. The more I thought of it, the more it nagged me.

Seven years later, in 1979, I went to my first boat show. I was quite impressed by the shiny new hulls, the long masts, and the new technology of it all. I was overpowered by intrigue and passion. I realized that there had been great changes in boats, but that the essence, the basics of sailing, had not changed. People still dreamed of sailing the world. I started to gobble up magazines on sailing. I first read about sailboards (surfing with a sail), but this was not for me. Then there came the era of light open sailboats, (dinghies) like lasers, mistrals, and sunfishes, to name a few. The more I read, the more I learned.

Life kept on sailing by, 5 years actually, and by 1984 I was still without a sailboat. I happened to be talking to one of my bosses when he told me that he had sailed a Fireball. They were about the fastest dinghy in their category, other than catamarans which were a double hull sailing craft. This impressed me. We talked about all kinds of boats that day, and on many other days as well. It struck a nerve in my system, like an electric jolt. I had almost forgotten about boats. I was so caught up in life's turmoil. I didn't see anything promising for me boating wise, in the near future.

I was a salesman working on commission in the field, selling housing renovation products for Sears. One day when I was out on one of my many calls, I was driving through St. Adele when I spotted this very tiny sailboat, a sixteen foot Invitation Bombardier, lying on a trailer. It was a bit rough but in solid shape. I stopped the car and sauntered over for a look. All it needed was a little elbow grease and some TLC, (tender loving care). There was nothing wrong with it that some paint and varnish couldn't fix. The sail was intact and everything was there, so I bought it 24 hours later. Money was one of the real problems I had to solve, and somehow I did. Later on that spring, I got to work on it and completely restored it in a matter of weeks. Not bad for a total of $1,700.

Jacinthe and I were anxious for me to take the boat out on its very first sail in Mont Tremblant Park. There was very little wind, but during the next hour I managed to make the boat fall over on its side and toss me into the water three times. I couldn't figure out at first why I kept flipping it over, and then I started catching on. I really started to enjoy it and have fun. For the rest of the afternoon it was precarious sailing. When Jacinthe and I took it out of the water to load it back onto the trailer, there were some curious visitors there from Japan who took pictures of the boat from all sides.

For the next three years, my wife, my daughter, the two boys, and I sailed this little jewel. One day, I decided to take my daughter on a long day sail across the Lake of Two Mountains. Halfway across the lake, the boom vang broke loose from the boom. The boom vang keeps the boom down close to the boat, keeps proper tension on the sail, and helps keeps the boom attached to the mast. We had our life vests on and I had attached a two foot long, one quarter inch diameter rope to the section of the boom that is attached to the mast, as a precautionary measure. I instructed Roxanne to wrap this rope around her hand to help her keep her balance when the boat shifted positions because of the wind or waves. For an eight-year-old, she was fairly brave. She had an unbelievable faith in her dad and I didn't want to let her down.

At one point after the boom vang broke loose, the boom and the sail shifted to a higher position. I didn't like the loss of control this caused. The boat was swinging from 0 to 20 degrees in jerky motions, lifting and heeling. The boom vang had been ripped out of its housing. I had an idea what to do and told Roxanne what I had in mind. At a certain moment, with her help holding up the boom vang in a certain way, I would let go of the rudder and lunge forward to grab the creature from her hand and plunge its little head into the second available hole, a slot just under the boom. This she understood, but all the while I was under great stress, anxious for my daughter's life and mine.

The wind was quite strong and I didn't want the boat to flip over … not there, away from any available help. We were two miles from shore in any direction. I checked the waves and wind and then turned the boat into the wind. On my signal to Roxanne, I lurched forward and grabbed the beastly creature and shakily shoved its head in the hole. I then turned the boat back to windward and pulled in on the sheet that pulled the boom back to its correct position. Everything was fine again. In a plastic bag hanging from the boom near the mast were my cigarettes and a lighter. That's where Roxanne was also handy. She passed me a cigarette and my lighter and I lit it and took a big drag. Ah… The rest of the day went beautifully. In the same bag we had a nice light lunch (gourmet style), a couple of baloney sandwiches, and two cans of pop.

My adventures multiplied. For my wife's first time sailing, we had prepared the boat for an afternoon of fun. My idea was to teach her the basics. I was in for a surprise. As we were getting ready to board, I asked her to sit in the front of the cockpit. As soon as she tried to get in the boat, and I mean *tried* to get in the boat, she started to scream very loudly. "What is it?" I asked. She said that the boat had moved and she thought that she was going to drown. "Oh, come on," I said, "sit in the boat." So again she tried to get in, but she was like a frightened puppy, and I wasn't even in the boat yet. I had forgotten that she was a very poor swimmer. Finally she got in. I told her to relax, that everything was going to be fine. As I pulled on the mainsheet, the boat heeled a bit, a bit too much for her, so she screamed bloody murder. Everybody up on this cement breakwater was looking down at us. I asked her to stop screaming because she was scaring the life out of me and told her that we weren't going anywhere until she felt completely safe.

A half hour went by as we practiced tiny sailing maneuvers in the small, protected, bay before she became willing to venture out. Then we crossed the lake, some two miles wide at this point. I explained to her that we were in the waviest area and that this was going to be fun. To my amazement, she bubbled with joy every time a wave came crashing onto the bow, getting her all wet. We sailed across the lake and back and then decided to stop for lunch. After a cigarette, she was ready to tackle it again. She was never frightened from that time on. Maneuvering a boat was quite another thing for her.

That same year my family and I went up to my mother's place at Lake Etchemin for our summer vacation. We brought our sailboat along to get in some sailing. The day after we arrived, my wife and I decided to go sailing. It was an overcast day and the wind was blowing pretty strong. The temperature was good, in the mid seventies. We donned our life jackets. My wife got into the front part of the tiny cockpit. I pushed the boat out and climbed into the back. I pulled in the mainsheet a bit and put down the rudder. Small sail boats have a retractable keel and a pivoting rudder, which kicks up when it hits the bottom in shallow water. This is a safety feature to help prevent damage to the boats and allow them to come closer to shore.

The retractable keel was in the upward position, so we began lowering it as we were leaving shallow water. It could reach down three feet; some keels can reach as far down as four feet. I barely had the boat set up when a huge gust of wind blew the boat onto its side. With no time to put my feet under the heeling straps, when the wind let up just as fast, I fell backwards and overboard. When I came up, my wife was still on the boat; but before she knew it, she was also thrown over the side. The boat made a circle and returned to its original position, and while my wife was still underwater, the boat passed over her and the keel rammed her leg. She came up above water panting for air, fearful and hurting. I told her to start swimming towards the sailboat, but neither she nor I could keep up with the boat, even though it was on its side, with one side sticking up three feet out of the water and the other side six inches below the water. We swam to shore slowly. I checked out her leg and found it was just a bad bruise but very tender.

All this time our daughter was watching us from her grandmother's porch. At one point she had lost sight of us and had started to panic. She cried, "They're gone! Do you have binoculars, Grandma?" Finally we surfaced, and she never stopped watching us until we were out of the water. Unbeknownst to us, some kind fellow saw our distress, and went out to fetch the sailboat. He towed it onto the public beach, but not without putting it upright first. We walked back to the house, and from there we brought the trailer to the beach, not really knowing where the boat was. To our surprise, the boat was right there, and the chap even gave us a hand putting it back onto the trailer.

That year being my first year, I continued to learn much about sailing and boat handling; things like how to capsize a boat on purpose and bring it to the completely upside down position, and then exercise the maneuver of bringing it right side up again and climb into the boat. Through personal experiences and books, I mastered the small art of sailing. I even got the boat to plane on the water – that was a scary feeling the very first time! I also made a jib, which gave the boat more speed. My boat wasn't designed for a jib, but I improvised, and what fun!

The next year I went to Oka Park on my own. I was preparing to sail, and I noticed that the wind was quite strong. There were a number of surfboard sailors out there, and they were flying. There were no other sailboats, just surfboarders. I was a bit leery about the situation, so I decided just to watch them for a while. It wasn't a sunny day, more of a grey, lonely, menacing day. I finally got up the courage to venture out. After all, it was only wind and water, and I did have my vest. So out I pushed the boat. I slid into the cockpit, feet under the heeling straps, keel board and rudder up. The water was shallow for the first twenty feet. Then down rudder, down with the movable keel, and the wind picked me up from behind like it had that day my wife and I had our spill in Etchemin, Quebec. The boat was moving out marvelously fast, and I had good control.

Then the waves grew to about one and one half feet, about twice the height of the boat. I figured I had better stay in close to shore – about three hundred feet or so out – as the sailboarders were doing. I decided to turn to starboard into the waves and wind to head back to the point where I had started, but the boat didn't have enough speed. I turned a bit to port and I let her rip for all she had, then I turned starboard into the waves and wind for a second time, trying to turn around, but the boat capsized. I was as quick as a rabbit. I never fell into the water. I jumped over the high side and stepped onto the keel. As the boat started to right herself, I jumped back into the cockpit. I realized that the wind and waves were too much, so I had to turn to port. This I didn't like because the wind could rip out the mainsheet and cause other damage, as well as perhaps some damage to me.

I tried a third time to turn into the wind and the hungry waves, but nothing doing. The boat capsized again and I fell into the water this time, but I didn't let go of the mainsheet. This became my lifeline, permitting me to swim around the boat. I stepped onto the keel and righted the boat again, climbed aboard, and set a tack. The waves could have rolled me over very easily, and that's why I was cutting through the waves at a slight angle; but I couldn't get enough speed to turn into them. Without speed, the boat would most certainly roll onto its side.

My last chance was to jibe, to turn away from the elements. I waited for the right spot on the wave and pulled on the tiller and crossed my fingers. As the boat began to turn, I saw that my timing was wrong. I had turned too soon. *Damn it!* Over I went with the boat. Still clinging to the mainsheet, I was caught with the boat between me and the waves. I pulled the sheet out of the jamb cleat and tried to swim around the boat to get to the keel. It was taking too much time, and my boat was starting to turn upside down. I finally got around the boat. With a great deal of difficulty, I finally was able to climb onto the keel, which was high out of the water. The sail and mast were submerged some 15 degrees.

I tried to set the boat upright but nothing happened. I tried again and again, but no progress. I sat on the keel, straddling it like it was a horse, wondering what to do next. The waves were pounding the hull like giant hammers, driving the top of the mast deeper and deeper into the sand at the lake bottom. Off to my right there was another sailboat with three men on board, and they were having exactly the same problem. My mast was stuck in the lake bed. You see, the mast was approximately twenty feet long, but the water depth was only ten feet, this being a shallow section of the lake. The shore was about 3/4 of a mile away. Finally, after ten minutes, which seemed like hours, the three men got their boat free and sailed away, abandoning me.

I was afraid. It could have been a matter of life or death for me. I sat there, straddling the keel, for at least an hour. I was getting cold, and I was out of ideas. Then I started to throw my weight up and down really hard onto the keel, thinking maybe I could free her this way. I was praying to God for some help. This went on for some time when ... crack! Suddenly, the boat turned to an upright position. I thought that the keel had broken.

Then my chin dropped to my knees. There before me stood the mast, or I should say, half of the mast. I had broken it in two and my sail had ripped in half and was shredded.

I quickly climbed aboard and headed for shore. It began to fly towards the shoreline like a wild stallion on the run. I had no sail, just a tattered, raging rag. But, with the wind beating against my back, it was more than enough to propel me back to the shoreline. Once there, I thanked the Lord for my good luck. With immense difficulty, I walked along the shore back to the trailer, towing my boat by hand. I noticed that the place was deserted. I felt sad and lonely, but relieved that I was alive. The next day I looked at my thighs. Ow! Both of my inner thighs were completely black and blue, not to mention sore and tender. I never did find out just how hard the wind had been blowing that day, but from then on I respected its fearsome strength.

On a camping trip in 1985, I removed the mast and sail from the sailboat and gave each of my three kids a paddle. I said to the kids, "You are a bunch of Indians, so paddle!" Boy, this was the greatest thing I could have done for them. We spent the next two hours just sitting there on a sixteen foot sailboat, all five of us, as they paddled their hearts out. What a wonderful day!

There were many other great times I got to enjoy with my family. As time went on, my wife and my three children had all learned to sail. There were many times when Marc, our youngest, and only five years old, held onto the same little rope as Roxanne had done, for he also came sailing with me. It was moments like these that I had always wanted to share with my own dad. Though he was irreplaceable, I was so afraid of my father. Now, being a father myself, I rather enjoyed being with my children, and this was important to me. With time, I gave them my dream, the art of sailing.

During a summer weekend at my mother's home, there was another fun incident. My brother and sister-in-law had joined my wife and me at Lake Etchemin for a couple of days. On one particular day, my sister-in-law wanted to go for a sail. "Okay, let's go," I said. The next thing I knew, we were pulling out of the bay as I was explaining the basics of sailing to her. When it was time to make a tack, she began to crawl under the boom to get to the other side of the boat as I was coordinating the sailing maneuvers. The shift of weight caused the boat to heel, and into the water we both fell. As we came up for air, we saw that the boat was on its side. I told her to grab hold of the dagger keel. All of a sudden, little, red things started to fly all around. I looked into the water and there they were her fingernails – fake fingernails! "Relaaaaax," I said, "This is the fun part of sailing." I told her how I was going to set the boat upright, and that went rather well. Then I asked her to climb back into the boat. No way! She didn't even get close to boarding. I said, "Okay, I'll climb in and help you get on board."

Her earlier graceful movements, like when we had turned about, were a sign of what was in store for us. I couldn't pull her onto the boat – not by her arms, not even by her legs. She was tall and well set, not a tiny baby, if you know what I mean, but a lot of woman. The only way I could figure out to get her back to shore was to tow her with a rope! I towed her to shore, right in front of a barbecue party. Imagine the people there all really having a ball watching us. No matter. She brushed the sand off her swimsuit, not disturbed in the least, got back in, and we shoved off again. We continued our sailing adventures and had a nice, fun day.

After sailing this little critter for three years, my heart began to yearn for a bigger boat, one with a cabin top and a heavy keel, a boat that was more stable and roomy … a real boat.

# 4. *Doulande* – The Tanzer

I read the "For Sale" ads for used boats regularly, but the boats were always too old, too expensive, or too big. I also started to look around marina yards that were within a radius of around four hundred miles. There were many lakes in the area. I went to boat shows in Montréal and Toronto. I also started reading a magazine called *Boats for Sale* and continued reading it for the next 20 years. I gobbled up each new issue like I was having a love affair, reading every word and looking at every picture four or five times, if not more. I would cut out articles and tape them into my scrapbook, along with pictures of all my favorite boats. I was convinced that there was a boat out there for me. I never stopped hoping and dreaming. I learned a lot reading this magazine and others.

One fall morning in 1986, I was driving to work in Montréal along the Metropolitan when, off to the side, I saw this twenty two foot Tanzer sitting in a cradle on a trailer. It was for sale. I couldn't take my eyes off her every time I passed by. I even stopped one day to see the boat close-up. I went to talk to the owner, who lived just across the street, to see where he stood on the sale price and left discouraged because I couldn't afford it. It wasn't all that much, but with a family, a home, and a business renovating kitchens and bathrooms and installing kitchen and bathroom cabinets which was not making any money. I just didn't have a chance.

Then one day as I got to my store, my wife's sister, who worked for me at the time, asked me if I was all right. "Oh," I said, "I keep having this dream, this wish to have a real boat someday; but there doesn't seem to be any way that I can achieve it." She told me that if I thought about it real hard, if I wished it hard enough, I could make it happen, it would come to me. I started to laugh. "That's too easy! If that were true, then everyone would do that." She said that it was true, but that nobody tries it. I shook my head in dismay.

On my way home from work I noticed that the boat was gone. My heart skipped a few beats. I drove off the highway and turned around and went back to where the boat had been. I saw that it had been moved to the owner's backyard. I glared at it in despair, and after a while, continued on my way home. I started wishing for it, started to really think about it.

Winter had come and was now nearing its end. One day I spotted an ad in a boating magazine about a 22-foot Tanzer. It was on the Richelieu River, not far from Noyan. I phoned for some details, and after I hung up, I started to think of ways to buy it. My only hope was my brother, who was 3 1/2 years my junior. He came down to Noyan with me, and we made an appointment at the marina with the couple who owned the boat.

We went directly to the boat, where the owners and a boat surveyor met us. There was over a foot of snow on the boat, but the sun was warming things up, our hearts included. There wasn't much to see there, just a dream filled with snow. We looked over the boat with the boat surveyor. We then drove to the owners' home, following them anxiously. Here we inspected the sails, motor, and the rest of the equipment. After we left, my brother and I talked a lot about the boat. I think he was now convinced that he also wanted a boat.

He worked out a way for us to buy it. He would pay the initial purchase price, and I was to reimburse him for my half of the boat in small installments. Jacinthe's sister had been right. I had wished it, and it had come true. I was grateful to my brother for the generous payment arrangements. We were now the proud owners of a twenty two foot sailboat, with twelve hundred pounds of keel. I was about the least wealthy man in the country, but I managed somehow to have part ownership of a real boat. I hadn't tried to convince my brother or persuade him. I had simply given him an idea, and he was very happy with the situation.

We began the work of preparing the boat for sailing. The first weekend we made it back down to the boat, we started by scraping the hull to remove the old antifouling paint. It was the 18th of April and the temperature soared into the low eighties; but after only two days, we had removed the old antifouling paint and the new antifouling paint was on. We made arrangements to rent a dock space at the Gagnon Marina on the Richelieu River and had her put in the water.

On the 5th of May, our wish came true. My brother, his wife and two sons, along with my wife, me and our three kids were all neatly packed into the cockpit. We started up the motor and left the dock, heading up the river towards Lake Champlain, some ten miles away. The day was grey and overcast with a slight chilly breeze, but in our hearts the sun was shining.

One hot day for the family on Douland

Checking out the ropes

I got up on the cabin top to check out the ropes, to get an idea of what we were in for. I remarked to my brother, "Boy, I think that Dad would have just loved to be with us." The irony of it all was that day; (the 5<sup>th</sup> of May) marked the anniversary of his passing away sixteen years earlier. In our hearts, we were thinking of our dad; we were sharing his dream.

Now here I was, learning all over again how to handle an entirely different kind of boat. The first time down the Richelieu River, it took my brother and me 1 ½ hours to motor to Lake Champlain. We had to pass by a railroad swing bridge. Since there were no trains in sight, the bridge opened up as we came into view. Next we had to wait at a lift bridge that handled a lot of traffic. Coming back in the evening on hot days, we would have to wait as long as two hours for it to open, which was quite annoying. The delays were so long on a number of occasions that we return to our dock in complete darkness.

All that year I sailed *Doulande* without taking a single navigation course. I did refer to the navigation charts. Talk about luck! Nothing dangerous ever happened except for a few scares on the odd occasion. On our first time out, we used too much sail and the water was coming over the side into the cockpit. It was a bit scary, but this had often happened with my other little boat; though it was new to my brother. This time we had heavy ballast, a metal keel to keep us upright. On another occasion, I was sailing the boat when a foghorn started to blow and I saw that someone on a boat far away was waving at me. He was doing that to make me aware that I was in shallow water. I now saw the boulders on the bottom of the lake, and so I turned the boat around, barely brushing up against one of the rocks. Phew! I waved back in appreciation for their help in warning me.

One fine summer day when there was a gentle wind, I decided to tow my son, Francois, a wiry 8 year old with a contagious smile. He was in his little vinyl dinghy, a gift from grandma. I secured his dinghy to a fifty foot line, which was all that was needed. All this was a lot of fun for him. Then the wind picked up ever so slightly, and then up another notch. Francois had the biggest smile on his face, but not for long. The wind picked up again, and since I had kept a sail up on the boat, the sailboat with the dinghy in tow started to go faster. Some water started to get into his dingy. Soon, the dingy was getting sucked into the water because of the faster towing effect. With a little more wind now, Francois, along with the dingy, were on the verge of being sucked completely down into the water.

Water was starting to fill the dingy. He hollered, and I released the tow line and shouted back at him not to panic. It took a few minutes to turn around and come to his rescue. Everything turned out just fine, but for a moment there, he was pretty shook up. This was another lesson learned, and there were more on the way. With sailing, the mistakes that you can make are akin to leaving food in your tent when you go camping. If you don't have any knowledge on the subject, these kinds of errors can create monstrous problems. School is never out in life.

My wife and I decided to take a one-week holiday with the kids and sail all over Lake Champlain. Two little problems arose. The first one came up when we arrived at Malletts Bay. There was no room at the marina, so we anchored out. We sailed over to a high cliff area which protected us from the wind as long as it continued coming from that same direction. After our supper we loafed around a bit, and then it was bedtime. The youngsters had the v-berth, and this pleased the three of them. It was like a camping trip. We had a good night's sleep. In the early morning light, we began to rise like freshly baked bread.

My daughter said, "Dad, there's no land around us."

"What?" I exclaimed as I got up in a hurry and looked out. She was right! We had drifted quite some distance, a mile maybe. Our anchor had slipped. Thank God there was no wind and we were in no danger. We pulled up anchor and motored into the marina for pump-out services and to stretch our legs. We docked for the day. There were ducks swimming around, and the kids had fun feeding them. Then we went for pizza. The kids were excited and I was as well. The food was better than the boat's cuisine thought the kids and it was a well-deserved rest for the boat's cook, my wife, Jacinthe.

Later in the evening my wife and I wanted to open a bottle of wine to celebrate our holiday, but we didn't have an opener. I went over to the neighboring boat, a beautiful sailboat some forty five feet in length. Sunlight was getting scarce, but I could see the artificial light that was beaming out from the hatch cover. As I was not familiar with the etiquette of visiting neighbors, I climbed aboard and knocked on the cabin top. The owner was a middle-aged curmudgeon, hostile and impolite. He asked me if I had any manners and where did I come from? I apologized and explained that, seeing that no one was on deck, I thought it would be all right to come on board and knock. I told him that all I really wanted was to borrow a wine bottle opener. A woman came up the companionway and handed me an opener. With a nice smile, she asked me to leave the opener on the deck when I was through with it. I was frustrated, but what could

I do? "Those Aristocrats"!!! I thought. "They embarrass you and make you feel cheap and uneducated! Maybe they're right." The next day I was with my kids feeding the ducks when the lady from the night before came over to me and apologized for her husband's behavior.

That same morning two officers on boating patrol wanted to inspect my boat for "safety reasons." I was sure the old coot had called them down. It was actually more for conformity reasons. All they found was that I needed a second fire extinguisher, laws being different from one country, province, or state, to another.

There was this middle-aged couple on another boat who were more down-to-earth. They were getting ready to head for Burlington, Vermont. I shared my concern with them that it was rather windy. I was going to the same place, but I was a bit leery with three kids. That was a lot of kids depending on me for their safety. A little later the man came by and mentioned that the weather was going to be stable for the day. I told myself that it must be all right to go if this couple was going, so we shoved off and sailed away. I had underestimated my assessment of the wind and of the talent of this upper middle aged couple. They turned out to be much better navigators then myself. My ego paid the price.

We came to a narrow passage that led us out of Mallets Bay and into Lake Champlain and sailed through it without a hitch. There was very little margin for error, but the wind was favorable for the direction we were heading. We had to sail around an island before we could proceed south towards our destination. It was like a complete calm before the storm. I had my largest sail set, and as we rounded the island, we caught the full force of the wind. I panicked. The boat was heeling way too much for my liking. My wife looked at me in silence and I asked the children to get inside the cabin and put on their life jackets. I then asked my wife to go forward and change the sails, but first she had to get this large sail down, and fast.

The poor girl couldn't stand up; she had to crawl on her back like a crab. I asked my nine-year-old daughter to open the front hatch from the inside and haul in the genoa while my wife lowered and unhanked the sail. All the while my stomach was in a knot. Once that was done, everything went smoothly. Roxanne passed Jacinthe the mid-sized sail, and once it was hanked and set, off we went. In the turmoil, my wife lost one of my favorite baseball caps, the one that had "The Expos" embroidered on it. I was really proud of my wife and daughter for their teamwork. We were out of danger, but the day wasn't over.

Later, we encountered three foot waves and strong winds. We came across a catamaran that had flipped over. The crew had plenty of help from two other boats, but we wished them good luck anyways. It's the hardest craft to turn right side up. Noticing big, black clouds coming our way, we brought down the mainsail and the jib and tied them down. I couldn't outrun the oncoming storm. Regardless, I started up the engine and we headed towards Burlington, which was a mile or so away. We were nearing the breakwater when it started to rain nails hard as steel, really cold ones. The wind was picking up, and to top it off, there was lightning.

We made it behind the breakwater, but to my surprise, the place was full of boats. This did not look promising. I finally found anchorage at the last minute with barely enough room between our boat and three other boats. I had Jacinthe drop the anchor and I shifted the engine into reverse to set the hook. It took two tries, all this amongst wind and rain. I had taken off my shirt before we even made it behind the wall, and now I was starting to get cold. With the hook set, we went inside the cabin and my wife prepared something to eat.

There was a tiny table for two adults or three kids on one side, and of course, the cook had the other bench. I sat behind her, drying myself with a towel. I started thinking about the day's adventure. Again my smart little girl said, "Dad, we're moving." I looked through the porthole, not believing her; but sure enough, she was right again. *Man!* Out we had gone into the storm and tried to anchor again. We had drifted some fifty feet or so and had just enough time to make the maneuvers to get back to a safe anchorage. What I had not realized was that the wind had changed direction. This was worrisome because it meant the anchor could unset itself. In general, two anchors are always much safer than one.

About an hour later the wind died down. Looking at my chart, I said to my wife, "Let's get out of this sardine hole and head down to Shelburne Bay." It was 7 nautical miles away. By the time we got there, it was getting dark. The place was full up, and the only anchorage available was outside of the protected perimeter. This time we had more room to let out more rode. Still I had to be sure that we wouldn't bump into some other boat if the wind died down. If there's wind, all the boats move in the same direction and have the same position. If the wind changes direction, the boats all move again in the same direction. However, when the wind dies down, it can get a bit chaotic; the boats can bump into one another, because they are all free to move about in any direction. I was a bit worried, so I went up on deck to see if we had moved. No, everything was fine.

The following day we docked at an old pier and went ashore to stretch our legs a bit and let our imaginations fill in the silence. Once back at the makeshift dock, we "set out to sea," as my children would always say. We had plotted our actual route from Plattsburg to Mallets Bay from the beginning of our trip in Plattsburg, recording our time and position every half hour. We had sailed some 50 nautical miles tacking back and forth to reach a point 14 nautical miles away! On days when the wind is with us, traveling in a strait line, we can cover a distance of 50 nautical miles. Assuming we are traveling six knots per hour, it takes 8 hours and 20 minutes to travel 50 nautical miles. All of this depends on the wind direction and water currents.

On our return trip from Shelburne Bay to Mallets Bay, I decided to take a shortcut between an island and the shore. The darkness was slowly creeping in, and we wanted to stay overnight at Mallets Bay one more time. The charts showed a depth of six feet with some areas as shallow as four feet. I didn't know that the actual lakes water level was one foot less than the chart depth, meaning there was only three feet of water where we wanted to pass, and the boat had a forty two inch draft. I was slowly motoring through this area when we got stuck in the silt and mud. I couldn't back up, so I let out the boom, and my wife, who is about the size and weight of a fly, gingerly moved out to the end of it and tried to make the boat heel to one side to hopefully cause the keel to lift free. We didn't need very much heeling, but no chance. Next, I got out of the boat and stood on the bottom of the shallow area of the lake and pushed the boat backwards as Jacinthe revved the motor in reverse. We finally set *Doulande* free. I climbed aboard and cleaned up as we slowly motored around the island in the opposite direction. We got to the bay in complete darkness and anchored out overnight.

The last two legs of our trip went without a hitch, except for when we were motoring along the Richelieu River. It was dark so I decided to turn on my spotlight. Disbelief! Sand flies by the millions invaded us, making it difficult to even breathe or talk. I turned off the spotlight and we had to use our own personal "night vision" our eyes, to get through. Finally, with yet another test behind us, home port came into sight. We slept at the dock that night and went back home the next day, all in all more mature and a bit wiser – and we did have lots of fun. The youngsters just loved every minute of the trip.

When sailing, the only times I was the least bit stressed was when I was with my brother or if I was alone. There was no worrying, and I could relax. I was always worried about my family when the wind was too strong or if we were miles from shore. I felt I might not be able to save them if we sunk or if someone fell in the water. Such situations were my ultimate nightmare.

This brings to mind one occasion when my family and I were coming back from a day of sailing. We were meandering up the river by motor when two heavy displacement cruisers, one following behind the other, started to overtake us on our port side, with the shoreline off to the right. They weren't going fast, but then again, they weren't going slow enough either. For cruisers, going slow and going slow enough so as not to leave a wake are two distinctly different things. Sailboats are very narrow compared to cruisers.

When we hit the first wake, which was at least three feet high, boy, did we bounce! Immediately afterwards, the second cruiser started to pass us slowly, but not slow enough. The second wake pushed us from behind at first, causing our boat to surf, and this brought us closer to the first boat. Then it lifted us high as the wake passed under us and dropped us. The children, who were inside the cabin, flew in every direction. The youngest smashed his head into the bulkhead and his foot came crashing down onto a tiny angle iron used to fix the dinette table, splitting open his heel. The other two were just banged up a bit – and I was very much in a panic. Losing control of a boat is a very frightening experience.

On another occasion, I and three other adults were on the *Doulande* and motoring out to the lake. As we approached the swing bridge, a cruiser started to pass us on our left. This was not the place to do so, but he did it anyways. The strong wake pushed our boat towards the column that supported the bridge. I tried to turn back, but there was no response from the rudder. I looked behind me and saw that the outboard motor had turned on me. I was in a panic! In just the nick of time, I turned the motor back around and pulled on the tiller to set us straight. That was a close call. I was fuming. I wanted to beat the living daylights out of this guy! And if he was too big, I wanted to shoot him with my flare gun! And if that turned out not to do the job, I wanted to make a barbecue out of his boat with him on it!

Then there was the time that my wife was the helmswoman for this occasion. I was in the cabin making a sandwich when we were being passed by a cruiser. It always happens on a river. She called out to me in a panic, and I answered her by saying, "Have confidence in your self!" She ordered Francois to help her steer. When the wake hit, they looked like fish floundering out of water. They never let go of the tiller, but boy, did they look funny! First my wife was standing, next she was flat on her rear, and finally she got back up and was flung from side to side. Needless to say, it's important for everyone's safety that cruisers exercise consideration when passing smaller boats. That year, 1987, was quite a year on the Richelieu River and Lake Champlain.

I could mention that we had many, many wonderful days sailing, swimming, tanning, reading and sleeping, and what else, all the good things that come with sailing. A boat is like a cottage. It's even better sight-seeing in a boat than in a car. There's more sharpness, depth, and clarity in the scenery. Oh, and you never have to cut the lawn.

# 5. Lake of Two Mountains/Oka

In 1988 I made arrangements to transfer the *Doulande* to Oka in the Lake of Two Mountains area. With my lumberjack of a stepfather whom had a heavy-duty pickup, and with a flatbed trailer that I had rented, we began to drive. It took 2 ½ hours to get to where the *Doulande* was docked at the marina on the Richelieu River. We arrived early and I started to prepare the boat for the trip to Oka. I had to dismast this thing, something I had never done before. When you're doing such a task by yourself, and it is the first time doing it, everything seems like a humongous chore. Some help would have been nice, but everyone was occupied, even the marina workers. My stepfather wasn't too keen on participating, I never knew why. He sat in the cab of his truck and waited. I finally got the mast down with a bit of help from a passing worker. At that point, my stepfather finally joined me and lent a hand. Now I had to lash down the mast so that it wouldn't move during the haul.

Next, the lift came to take the boat out of the water and place it on the cradle, which was chained down to the trailer. A cradle is very heavy; you don't pick it up or move it around like a toy. You need another lift of some sort, such as a portable boom or tractor with a shovel or scoop, to move it. Once the boat was in place, I scrambled for the next hour tying and taping and securing the mast properly over the boat. The boat needed to be strapped to the trailer as well.

By the time we were ready to leave, it was already late afternoon and it was rush hour in Montréal. We were caught in it right up to our ears. It was stressful having this huge whale-like body following behind us. It appeared menacing and frightening, as if it was just waiting for a chance to pounce on us! We got to Oka at around 5 p.m., just in the nick of time to have the boat unloaded and it was a race against time getting the trailer back to the rental company in Montréal to avoid having to pay for another day.

Boating can be much more costly than you would imagine. Lift cradle onto trailer = $$$. Lower mast onto boat = $$$. Lift boat out of water and have it placed onto trailer = $$$. Rent trailer = $$$. Hire a driver and pay for truck rental and gas = $$$. Pay for another lift to have the boat taken off the trailer and set into the yard = $$$. Ulcers however, are free.

While on the subject of costs, let's see what other surprises were in store for us. Antifouling, wax, oil, new ropes, repairs, tune-up, and gadgets to pretty up the investment, such as boots, life jackets, scrub brushes, mop, pail, cleansers, varnish or teak cleaners, cushions … the list goes on. As the years add up, so do the repairs and fixings and replacement of items. Did I mention insurance, and tarps or shrink-wrap, and dock fees, and winter storage?

Once I got through all this, I was a little dizzy; but I got it done. Now you know why there are so many divorces or separations in the sport of boating. Surprisingly, I was still married after all this. My wife was taking it in stride, with good patience.

I was ready for another season of sailing. I was ready to feel the wind blowing softly on my face and in my hair and to feel the sunshine painting my body so that I looked like a seasoned mariner, all ruffled and tanned – not without a few more scars added to the list though. I was becoming more of an authority with each sailing season.

One day I was sailing with my brother and our wives. Nice sunshine, 8 to 10 knot winds; everything was perfect. There were lots of boats on the sparkling water. They all looked like butterflies gliding across fields of diamonds. We were going upwind on a port tack, with nobody nearby. We had the 150% (50% bigger than the mainsail) genoa set. With a list of 10 to 15 degrees, we were gliding along beautifully. There was a plastic window in the genoa to help us see ahead, but our view was still very limited. We made a starboard tack, and then a port tack 10 minutes later. We were passing through a narrow section near Parsons Point, and the tacks were necessarily frequent now.

All of a sudden my brother yells out, "There's a boat to starboard!" I looked under the genoa to see this sailboat, some one hundred feet or so away, coming straight for us. Since I was sitting on the starboard side, I pulled hard on the tiller and made a fast turn to port, changing from a port tack to a starboard tack. The other boat woke up at the last minute and also made a turn to his port and changed his starboard tack to a port tack. We must have missed each other by only six inches … we may have actually touched one another. We looked at each other in disbelief.

I then made a three hundred and sixty degree turn in order to continue on our same heading west. At that same moment, the other boat was making the same move, unbeknownst to me; he was long gone as far as I was concerned. But here we were again on a head-on collision course, and this time it was too late. We made a connection, his bow just glazing the aft quarter on the starboard side of our boat.

I yelled at him, "What are you up to?"

He replied in the same tone, "Where do you think you're going?"

It took me a while before I realized what had I done wrong. Boats are not regulated like cars. Boats can wander all over the water, and stop signs and traffic lights don't exist. There are no boundaries. There are just a few rules, and they apply equally to all the different kinds of boats. My first mistake was I hadn't been scanning the horizon enough. Next, during my navigation classes with the Canadian Power Squadron, I'd learned the rules concerning the right of way. One of the rules applies to motorboats and sailboats. When a sailboat is involved with a motor boat, the sailboat has the right of way 99 % of the time, when under sail. This is because a powerboat can maneuver around a situation much more easily, and a sailboat must have much more space and time in which to react.

There's a different rule regarding the right of way for two or more sailboats. The boat that is on a starboard tack (the one that receives the wind from the starboard side) has the right of way, as opposed to the one that is on a port tack. Someone must yield, and that's the rule. I was on a port tack, and I was obliged to yield the right of way. A second rule comes into play when both boats are on a starboard tack; the boat that is upwind must yield the right of way. The third rule is if you're the captain of the boat with the right of way and you see that the captain of the other boat is not reacting, don't wait. React! It's better to move out of the way than it is to be dead right! In the confusing situation I was in, I had reacted and so had the other captain.

We were both lucky that day, as no damage was done and no one was hurt. I had performed the same maneuver the other captain had, thinking that his boat was gone. It's so funny how things happen sometimes. Anxiety and anger flared up, but just for a moment. I learned an important rule, and it has served me well on many occasions. Take a navigational course with The Canadian Power Squadron or an equivalent maritime organization.

It's fun and helpful. However, sometimes the rules are of no use. There are some boaters who will put you to the test. They don't get out of your way, because they don't know the rule or they just want you to move out of their way. Never insist on being dead right; move out of *their* way!

On one outing, my family and I were sailing under ideal conditions. We had been heading in a westerly direction for about three hours, cutting through 1-foot waves. Every so often, a wave would splash overboard, so I eased up on the mainsheet to slow us down a bit to make it more comfortable for us during a lunch of sandwiches, cheese, cookies, and a thermos of hot coffee.

Then we decided to turn back so we made a 180-degree turn and continued on our way. Now there seemed to be very little wind, so I told my wife that we were going to hoist the spinnaker. This is the sail that looks like a big balloon on the front of the boat. This was only my second time setting up this type of sail. Jacinthe was at the tiller, and I could've used a third hand. It took a little time, but up she went. I added a spinnaker pole; it helps keep the sail at the right height and distance from the boat, as well as maintaining its placement in regards to the wind. We were well under way. I explained to Jacinthe how to keep the sail in alignment with the wind and boat, and she mastered it quite well.

There was about a mile or more of water up ahead, so there was no need to worry. I asked Jacinthe to tell me if another boat came our way. I should've said that the same goes for buoys. I sat down in the cockpit with my back against the bulkhead, facing the helmswoman. There was a bright, hot sun shining down on us. Since we were going in the same direction as the wind, it was as if there was no wind. I had almost dozed off when, "pif, paf, bing, bang, boom!" We had hit something hard.

The boat jumped into the air and then came to a complete stop. We were heeling quite badly to one side and the waves were coming close to the edge of the cockpit. The sails were flapping violently, giving off such a deafening noise that it was frightening. I jumped up and saw that Jacinthe was fine. I turned around to look in the cabin. The children were fine as well, though they were in a bit of a panic. Marc had been banged about, having been flung forward into the inner bulkhead separating the compartment that he was in, from the front cabin. The other two were lucky because they happened to be sitting with their backs against the bulkhead. There was no water coming in.

I released the two sheets from their cleats, which brought immediate relief to the boat and to the two sails that had been whipping violently in the wind. The boat straightened up some, making it easier to work on. I looked around and saw that we were in no immediate danger. What I didn't like, though, was that there was a green buoy some one hundred feet behind us. This meant that we had passed on the wrong side of it. We were sitting on top of a rocky reef called Crow's Point (Pointe aux Corbeaux). Jacinthe, Roxanne, and I hauled in the two sails as a team.

Now that everything was secured, I tried to think of ways to get us out of this predicament. There weren't many. The boat was too high, and too much out of the water. There was one danger, and that was that the waves kept hitting the hull, causing the boat to rock so that the cabin was getting closer to the water. I didn't like this one bit. I didn't have a V.H.F. radio on board, so I decided to use the only tool I had to call for help, the fog horn. I scanned the horizon to see if there were any boats in the vicinity, and I could see none. I blasted the horn three times. With no one in sight, every five minutes I again blew the horn three times. Then I spotted this powerboat passing by in the far distance. I blew the air horn three times, but the power boat kept getting further away. I was feeling pretty discouraged when suddenly, there he was, turning around and coming straight towards us.

As it approached us from behind, the other captain and I hollered out a plan of attack to each other. As he was slowly maneuvering in front of me, to get positioned to tow me out, he struck a rock. That had not been a good idea. Luckily, there was no damage done. I proposed that he come as close as he could to the stern, and we would attach a tow rope between the two of us. After a couple of tries, the tow ropes were tied together and in place. I started my engine. With my engine in reverse and him pulling us, we tried to back out. I had my two favorite flyweight sailors, Jacinthe and Frank (Francois), on the boom to transfer the point of gravity more to port, helping to raise the keel a bit. The rope broke loose. We tried again, and with a little perseverance, we got off the rocky bottom. In safe waters now, I was glad that it was over. I thanked the gentleman for his help, and I promised myself that from then on, I would help anyone else in need. A helping hand in a moment of crisis was welcome indeed.

We motored back to the marina in a kind of hypnotic state. I needed time to think about this. I explained to Jacinthe why this had happened, and this made her, and all of us, better sailors. A captain is supposed to know his crew's weaknesses, and the crew is a reflection of the captain. Another maritime lesson: always pass on the proper side of a buoy. One side is the safe side. The rule is, "red right returning" in North America.

It means when returning from the oceans, keep the red buoys to your right while you're traveling inland. Upon entering a marina or docking area, the same rule applies. This is where I had failed. If I had seen the buoy, I would have had her navigate to the left of the green buoy, or let the green buoy pass to the right (starboard side) of the boat, because we were going downstream (back towards the ocean). I hadn't realized that we had traveled so far in such a short time. I should have looked at the chart instead of relying on my memory. If I had, I could have prevented this ordeal. After sorting all this out, we all went and had that famous lunch, the greatest hotdogs around, *Lemieux Hotdogs*, slightly burnt, with relish, mustard, and onions, served on toasted hotdog buns, along with Coke or Sprite and coffee.

I returned the favor later on by helping another sailboat captain in a similar predicament. He was stuck high on a rocky shoreline. I kept my sailboat outside the area and set anchor. From there, I swam towards his boat. The water was a shallow three feet deep. I pulled the topsail halyard, which was attached to the top of his mast, while I waded out into the water some distance from his boat, causing the boat to heel, and we got her off the rocks. It felt so good helping someone.

The weekdays didn't go by fast enough. I was always anxious to go out sailing again. I sometimes thought that maybe there was time for an evening sail, but it wasn't worth the trouble with so little time. This was one problem, and the second was finding someone to go with on short notice.

One thing I hated was sailing on a hot, humid day and having the wind die down on us. We would start to cook in the sun, so we would lower our sails and set up our tiny, silky, red sun tent, which took 10 to 15 minutes. Our sun tent was not as good as a bimini top, but it helped. Then we'd motor to a safe spot, lower the ladder, and go for a dip. Sometimes our favorite spots were so far away that we would just head back to the marina and go swimming in the pool. We weren't the only ones. When the winds picked up again, not many boaters were motivated to venture out again on such a day.

One Saturday afternoon Francois and I went out sailing. I invited him not only as my son but as a sailing companion as well. When you're alone, it's difficult to maneuver in and out of a marina. Being two makes it much easier. Out on the water, it's easy to handle a boat by oneself; but in a marina on a windy day, it is like running after calamity. Out of her slip and down the waterway she glided, turning left in front of the service dock and then right once past the end of the last dock. Out into the breeze we headed and then started to prepare the sails.

Francois was a good sailor. He was the helmsman and I became the deckhand. As a matter of fact, I've always preferred being the deckhand, as there's more action. Mainsail up and set, up came the motor, which was mounted on a special bracket on the transom of the boat. Then to the front of the boat I went, setting the jib so it was ready to hoist. I then walked back to the mast and hauled her up by her halyard. I went back to the cockpit and pulled in the jib sheet to give it a tight, partially flat shape. The boat jumped to a faster speed, with a little more list. The boat had harnessed the wind, and the wind drew the sail in a forward direction, pulling the sailboat along. We were where we wanted to be, on the water, feeling the wind in our faces.

There was this twenty five foot Tanzer called the *Ugly Duck* passing us by as they were going in the opposite direction, so I ordered the helmsman to turn about and pursue the culprit. With a stronger wind, and on a port tack, we had increased our heeling and then, kabang, kaboom! I looked inside the cabin and there it was. A large toolbox had spilled all of its contents onto the floorboards, along with a leftover cup of coffee. It had not crossed my mind to check that everything was secured inside the cabin. Well, for the moment, I ignored it. We had more important business at hand – showing them we were no slobs to tangle with.

Slowly, we caught up to them, and both crews trimmed their ships' sails to go faster. We had a race on our hands! We were bow to bow for some time in a no-win situation. Then the sailors on the other boat noticed that there was a 10-year-old boy steering our boat. The lady helmswoman on the other boat gave my young son a nice smile and off we slid by ourselves into the wild blue yonder. I still think the helmswoman let up just a bit to let Francois take the lead. There's one thing I know for sure; Francois wore a big joker smile on that day.

Often we would anchor in a bay or in front of a public beach to just laze around, swim, read, and sunbathe. These were relaxing times. I tried to take a little nap in the cabin once in a while, but I was always stressed that the anchor might slip. I did manage some sleep in the cockpit, which was more than all right. Hearing the children laughing and playing always put me in a good mood. I called this sailing as well.

# 6. Toronto Bound

Around January 1989, I was in hot water financially with my business. I was afraid of a possible bankruptcy, so I gave back my unpaid half of the boat to my brother. In the spring of 1989, my brother moved the boat to Lake Ontario and docked it at Ajax near Oshawa. I went to Ajax for a week's vacation that summer to see my brother and his new home and business setup. We had planned to sail that week on Lake Ontario.

The first time out sailing with my brother and his wife, there were four foot swells. The ride was wonderfully smooth, not like the choppiness we'd encountered on the smaller lakes we had sailed on. It was like gliding over rounded waves. We had a lot of fun that day. Everything went well; no strong winds and no surprises either. The breeze was silky soft with a warm, sunny touch, It caressed our bodies, massaging and relaxing us. It was such an agreeable day, like an elixir, the kind that you wanted more of.

Two days later, by the looks of the tree tops, there was wind. The branches were bending over unwillingly as the leaves fought with the air to maintain their places. My brother and I packed our bags and went sailing with our wives. We arrived at the marina in the early afternoon and started to set up sail. The wind was puffing a bit hard, but it was nothing to worry about. Once the small sail and the reefed mainsail were set in place, we motored out of the channel. The wind, unobstructed now, was a bit stiffer. We hoisted the sails and away we went. Even with a stronger wind, a boat will perform well under the proper sail size. When in shallower waters, like those of Lake St. Francis, the waves are harder and choppier. We sailed into five foot swells, but they just rocked us like a baby. That was another agreeable afternoon.

My third time out was with my brother and his babysitter. We sailed into rougher waters than we had the previous day. We rose up on seven; even eight foot swells and slid down the other side, wave after wave. The boat shook about some, so much that we sent our guest inside the cabin for safety reasons. The waves crested, and the water was beginning to spray from wave crest to wave crest. We were a bit concerned at first, but after a half hour or so our nerves calmed down and we got to enjoy the sailing for the rest of that afternoon. This was one of my most exciting sailing experiences. Other than this trip, I had a sabbatical year from sailing. Sailing on Lake Ontario is a truly exhilarating experience that all freshwater sailors should have.

In 1989, I began thinking about sailing to faraway places like the Galapagos Islands and the islands of the Caribbean. I read stories such as one about a taxi driver in France who, on the spur of the moment, bought a sailboat and spent his summer training and preparing for a trip around the world. It was unbelievable what he went through. I laughed throughout the whole book. This taxi driver had to be nuts. One time he almost sailed into a reef while he was sleeping. Another time he found himself sinking in the Indian Ocean, thank God a freighter was passing by and the crew helped him. There were numerous other crazy adventures in this saga.

I read other interesting stories of men and women who travelled by sailboat. There was Tania Abel who crossed the Atlantic on her 26-foot Contessa; Bernard Moitessier, Eric Tabarly, Isabel Autessier, and Ellen McArther; Canadians like Jerry Roof and Michel Birch, who raced around the world; and what about the Canadian born American, Joshua Slocum, with his sloop, the *Osprey*, great reading, and it didn't stop there. I spent years reading and planning and dreaming.

In 1990 my brother returned the *Doulande* to The Lake of Two Mountains. That year, there was the Oka Indian uprising. We barely went to the marina for fear of some kind of reprisal. This was spoiling our summer, so we moved the sailboat to a marina called Presqu'ile Marina on the same lake but in a safer area. We stayed there for two seasons before we moved the *Doulande* back to Oka in 1992.

That year I suffered two heart attacks and lost my job because of too much absenteeism due by my health. I went back to school to learn a new trade, drafting. There I was, 50 years old, sitting at a school desk with men and women between the ages of 20 and 40. To qualify for this program, I had to take Grade 12 Equivalency Exams. Can you imagine me taking exams in math, English, history, economics, and geography? I was worried though. I had to do a bit of studying. The exams were in English and my English was getting a bit rusty. Thankfully, I passed the exams with flying colors, with nothing below 88%.

This drafting course to be my new trade lasted 56 weeks, and the hardest part for me was learning to use a computer. I was the most confused person in my computer class. I learned to use the AutoCAD (computer aided design/drafting) program plus many more programs, including Windows, Excel, and Word; and I had to learn all these new words and expressions that made up computer terminology.

There was another challenge here: I had attended school in Ontario where English was spoken, and this course was given in French, as I was now in Quebec. I had never learned to read and write French growing up, though I had learned to speak French at home with my parents. I was self-taught through reading newspapers and books, and I had taken a short French course to help me along. I had been living in Quebec for the last 25 years, and this had educated me as well. This was the deal. There were no other options for me. When the teacher talked in class, I couldn't afford to be distracted for a second. I was falling behind in my computer class. I could have pulled the hair out of my head. I finally bought a computer so I could practice on my own time. I didn't have the money, but if I was to succeed, it had to be done or my goose was cooked. I really felt stupid and annoyed those first three months. Well, it all paid off in the end. Thirteen months later, out of a class of twenty one, ten of us passed, myself included.

This was a time in my life when, at the beginning of my first year, I was taking classes in the same high school that my daughter and two sons were attending, all at the same time. I came in at 3:30 p.m. and my kids would salute me on their way home. Most embarrassing! I think the kids probably felt my pain. This is all behind me now, for I have done much since with not the least regret. A whole year passed in which I barely saw my kids and my wife. I was privileged to see my wife during the day until 1 pm, and then she would leave for work. I got to see my kids only on the weekends, tough times. I couldn't have felt lonelier.

I became obsessed with the idea of travelling the globe after my heart attack. I always wondered what it would be like to be continually meeting new people from different cultures, with different beliefs, and who were just plain different. I thought, *I am part of this world, and I can't believe that I shall someday die ignorant of what there is all around me.* Sure, I had read books, seen documentaries, and met people at conferences who lived this life with their children and wives, and some who lived it as loners. I would often look at a globe and show myself or someone else all these special places of which I daydreamed.

I decided to do it. It became my goal. Island hopping was the safe way to go to take the time to discover this world of mine. I kept reading and reading and I started preparing myself for the day. With approximately seven years of navigational courses, I set the timer for 2000. I would be 55 by then. In regards to my boat preparations, it took from 1997 to 2004, four years past my deadline. I continued doing all the right things. There was only one hitch: my soul was mortgaged. I was tied to a cornerstone, and it was impossible to leave now.

# 7. Lake St. Francis/The St. Lawrence River

My brother and I moved the *Doulande* to Valleyfield, Quebec, on Lake St. Francis and it was docked there from 1993 through 1995. I had many, many more agreeable sailing days with my family, my brother and his wife, and our friends.

In the early spring of 1993, my brother and I made the preparations to move the *Doulande* to Campi Marina in Valleyfield. I got a hold of the charts needed and I began to plan a route with time estimates and compass references. We had to negotiate three lakes, a channel, and a sixteen mile canal, along with the Beauharnois Seaway Locks. My brother, my fourteen year old son, Francois, and I started out at 7 am. It was cold, so we wore tuques and winter coats. The sun was out though, and that helped. We left Oka and crossed the Lake of Two Mountains and motored into Lake St. Louis via the St. Anne's de Bellevue locks. We had a short wait for the locks to open.

Once on the other side of the lock, we tied the *Doulande* to a public dock and stopped for coffee in this quaint little town called St. Anne that had lots of restaurants, although breakfast didn't seem to be their specialty. Sixteen years later and I still think of this charming place. I'd love to move there and possibly write a book someday on love and romance maybe and how we act so foolishly sometimes, even at great risk, to live out our passions. After hoofing it for a while, we finally found a place where we could have breakfast. We stocked up our bellies and headed back to the boat and continued on our trip.

We zigzagged through a number of channels and buoys, clearing the most dangerous part of our trip. Passing Windmill Point, we prepared to encounter seagoing ships, big ones. We stayed clear of them as much as possible. You see, they don't have brakes. It takes them a mile to stop, so every move is calculated well in advance; and that's why it's compulsory for them to have pilots on board. Once we reached the Beauharnois Locks, we waited patiently for the green light. Next to a Canada Steamship boat passing through, boy, did we look small!

It was our turn to slip into the locks. The workers dropped us two lines, which we grabbed onto and wrapped around the forward and aft cleats of our boat to hold it in place. The water started rushing into the lock at such a rapid rate that it was spooky. The boat kept drifting out, away from the walls, and we had to continually tighten the lines as they became loose. Once up, we were level with the upper section of the locks. It was uncanny. The locks opened up and out we motored and continued through the canal. There was a stiff two knots of current that we were heading into. At a boat speed of six knots and subtracting two knots of current, we were traveling at four knots. This meant that it would take four hours just to get through the canal. Along with the distance we had already covered that morning, it turned out to be a long day.

I could see that we were going to use up all the fuel in our fuel tank, so we motored until the tank ran dry. I had to let the boat drift while I transferred the fuel from my jerry can to the portable fuel tank in the fuel compartment. To do this, I had to disconnect this tank and place it on the deck for the fuel transfer. Back into the locker went the fuel tank, and we started up the engine again. The boat had drifted safely to the center of the canal during this ten minute exercise. I started to compute the time it would take to finish the run. Then I estimated the amount of fuel it would take. My computations told me that we would be dry by the time we arrived in Valleyfield.

Once out of the canal, we had to cross Lake St. Francis and motor up the last section of water to the marina. The gas gauge was dropping, and the stress level was rising. Finally, there they were: masts, tons of masts, tall ones, short ones, all sizes, all about the place. We were finally there. We docked and I checked the gas tank. It had about a half quart of gas left. That was a bit too close. We could've sailed the last stretch of the lake; I don't know why we hadn't thought of that. I guess you had to be a sailor to think of that. Our E.T.A. (estimated time of arrival) was quite accurate but our fuel estimate was way off. Well, we made it, and our designated driver was there waiting for us.

That same summer, my wife and I had the opportunity to take a ten-day vacation sailing the *Doulande*. We were going to sail up the St.

Lawrence River to the town of Kingston. No kids, just the two of us. The object was to have no parental responsibilities on board. Above all, I wanted to stay clear of as many responsibilities as possible. It being just the two of us would be quite palatable, if not savory and spicy.

As we prepared for our departure, the list of things to do was endless. The weather was menacing. One thing led to the next, and four days later we were still at the dock. We decided to repair the compass, from which the alcohol had drained. I gave some thought to the problem and conjured up a solution. We went to a drugstore to buy some rubbing alcohol along with a syringe. Then we bought a tiny drill bit from the hardware store. We drilled into the bubble through the top and then injected the alcohol with the needle. Once it was full, we patched the little hole with some putty. It worked for a couple of days, until the plastic bubble cracked and broke into a million pieces. I do not recommend repairing a compass this way. Sometimes I wonder if I think too much.

Friday, on the 5th day, we motored out of Campi Marina and headed southwest. The weather had improved. I explained to my wife that in foul weather, captains usually stay in port, only venturing out when the weather improves. If caught in foul weather while at sea, then they make do. I broke an old, cardinal rule, and that was "Never leave on a Friday," it's very unlucky. Another old rule was "Women are not allowed on board because it causes mayhem amongst the men," but I was lucky, no trouble there. Finally, there was to be "no whistling on board, because it riles up the winds." My wife was very good at whistling. We didn't have the best weather for that time of year. I wondered if perhaps my wife had been whistling when she was out of earshot.

A sailor has reached his destination when his sails are set, so off we went. We arrived at a place called Creg's Key Marina and stayed there for an overnight sleep. After our breakfast, we pulled out of the marina and continued on our course up the river. The passage from Valleyfield to Cornwall is called Lake St. Francis, but actually it is part of the St. Lawrence River. There are numerous shallows and hidden reefs here, but you'll be safe if you follow the charts. When sailing, you must rely on every navigational aid you have; this includes landmarks, island placements, and channel buoys. Even your ship's compass is important. Sometimes it's tricky until two or more navigational elements are in place. One is generally not enough.

Cornwall was very pleasant. The marina had a beautiful park like atmosphere with picnic tables and barbecues and trees and grass everywhere.

The docks were all new and the clubhouse was in pristine condition. We stayed only one day and moved on the following morning. We arrived at the Eisenhower Locks early in the morning. We didn't have to wait long. Their system was so much better than any I had ever seen. They had floats that slid up and down the wall. We just tied ourselves to them and floated up with them. The elevation was quite high, so two locks were needed.

Once the second lock opened, we released the cables and started motoring away after the okay was given by the lock master. Did I forget to mention that we were towing a dingy? At this moment I turned my head to give some slack to the dingy when the lock attendant shouted to me. We were heading back towards the lock wall. I pushed so hard on the tiller that the crosstree hit the cement lock wall. Boy, I was shaken up there for a few seconds. There is always something lurking, waiting to get at you when you least expect it. I straightened out my ship's heading and we were on our way.

We motored to Chrysler Park Marina and docked for the day and took a tour to learn about some Canadian and American history. There was a battle that took place there during the War of 1812. I am always learning something new in regards to history when I travel about in Canada. Chrysler Park Marina was impeccable. They even had a free shuttle service to visit Frontier Town and a cemetery for the soldiers who had fought and died in the War of 1812-1814. We also visited a square-rigger, *The Fair Jean,* which took on "trainees" to give them a taste of life lived on board.

Next day we left by motor, continuing towards Kingston. We crossed a wake that was left by a tugboat heading in the opposite direction. I called out to my wife to hang on, that we were going to hit a big wave. Splish, splash, paff! This was not a wave, but a wall of water two feet high and not an inch less! It hit us so hard, it felt like we had rammed into a brick wall. Boy, do those tugs displace water! As I said before, there is always something lurking out there, waiting to catch you by surprise. You're never at ease when you're on a boat. You must stay alert at all times.

Arriving at the town of Prescott, we came into the marina. To my surprise, there was someone there to greet us at the dock, a girl whom helped us to tie up. We went in to register, and there were only girls there also. This was a municipal marina, and they had an all-girl staff that was very professional, helpful and considerate. We will always remember the warm and friendly welcoming we received. The marina itself was another well manicured place, clean and tidy. Most municipal marinas are more than well looked after.

We jumped ship and went for a walk around town. We had some ice cream to cool off. This place kind of reminded me of Welland, with its long, clean streets that were almost deserted. We visited a block house and learned more about the War 1812-1814, and Canadian-American history. I bought a book called *Merry Hearts Make Light Days,* which is based on the journal kept by a British soldier named John Le Couteur, in which he recorded his experiences during the War 1812-1814. It was very interesting indeed. I couldn't put it down until I had finished reading it. If you're a Canadian history buff, you must read this. It talked of many places where I had lived as a youngster and yet had no idea that there was such history there, aside from that of Sir Isaac Brock. A few years later by chance I was to explore, Fort Erie and the role that it played during the War 1812-1814.

We had stayed two days in Prescott and it was time to consider our next move. Either we could rush to Kingston and then head back immediately upon our arrival there, or we could stay an extra day in Prescott and start back at a more relaxed pace. We chose the second option, seeing that the weather had stolen five days of our holiday. The return trip went by without a hitch. We stayed in the same places we had stayed at, when we started our trip away from home, such as Chrysler Park and Cornwall.

We made our preparations to sail the last stretch of 20 some odd miles across Lake St. Francis to Valleyfield. We had a good trailing wind that moved us right along. We came across another couple on their boat, beating into the wind. They were so excited about the strong wind they even tried to convince me to put up more sail. I was content going at a smoother clip with my reefed main and my 100% genoa. I'd rather sail comfortably than stress myself for nothing. We still made good time crossing the lake. Once we had reached the other side of the lake, the swells started to get bigger. Behind us, the water rose higher than our boat after we had crossed its wave. It made us a bit anxious, but it was fun. We were hoping that the swells wouldn't affect our maneuvering between the buoys as we entered the port. There were a number of shallow, rocky spots, and the distance between the buoys was not very wide. A number of folks got hung up here in this maze for different reasons, but we made it through all right. It was now time to go home and see the kids.

With time, I got to be a much better sailor. There were some hard lessons and some not so hard ones, but school wasn't finished for me. One day when my brother and I sailed out on a much too windy day, I told him that it might be wiser to turn back. The boat had drifted too much to one side, sending us towards the shallow waters. I tacked quickly to port, hoping that we would make some headway out of this predicament, but no such luck. We were stuck within this narrow, treacherous section of the lake. My mistake was not motoring out farther before setting our sails.

We had only one chance to make our way out of this area. I told my brother that we had to make a controlled jibe. This meant we had to turn with the wind behind us on one side of our sail; then, as we turned, the sail would cross over from one side of the boat to the other. The wind, with its full force on one side of the sail, would begin pushing against the sail's other side. This was dangerous because it could injure someone on deck or throw someone overboard. A sail could rip open. The mast could even snap and fall over, leaving us in a state of havoc. Well, as we turned, it happened … rrriiipppp! The sail took a hard hit. It tore about ten feet down the seam. I hadn't been able to control the sail's speed when it crossed over. We managed to keep control of the boat and return safely to port.

On our way into the harbor, I came across a friend, who was leaving in his 26-foot Contessa. I asked if he was really going out in that mess. He answered, "Why not?" I mentioned that the weather was getting foul and we were facing an eastern front. "Winds from the east bring the beast." Was I stressed? You bet! But not my friend; he continued on his way.

Arriving at our dock, we tied up and talked for a while in the cabin. The wind growled even more, and then lightning started to lash out. The rigging started to sound like guitar strings being played, and the visibility was nil. It felt like the world was coming to an end. A few days later, I came across my friend and asked him how he had made out. Alive obviously! He said that it had got pretty hairy, and that he was alone at the tiller for at least two hours. His guests, for whom it was their first time sailing, were completely frightened and crying. All the while he was describing the events, he was smiling sarcastically as though it had been a fun experience. I didn't doubt that it had, but it wasn't right to have had it at the other people's expense. This was really annoying.

Later this fellow ran smack dab into a yellow anchorage buoy. Now these things are quite big and made out of steel, so how come he didn't see it? He said that the charts showed safe water everywhere. He hadn't noticed that there were four of these buoys and that they formed the four corners of a square and were spaced one mile apart from one another. The big cargo ships anchor amongst these buoys if there's too much traffic in the locks. Perhaps this was some kind of payback to this guy for taking the couple out in the storm.

One day a couple from Oka showed up with their sailboat. They wanted to sail Lake St. Francis. We chatted for some time over coffee and hamburgers. The weather wasn't up to par, so they decided to hole up until the next day. Then they were off. We crossed their path two or three days later on the lake. The man asked me if I knew what the horns or whistles coming from another boat meant. I told them yes and asked why he had asked. He related this incident where a large cargo ship was blowing its horn at him. He decided to cross its path and then realized his error. The ship was coming towards him much faster than he had anticipated, and he had to start up his motor to get out of the way.

I explained to him that large containers or any cargo ships always have the right of way. The navigation rule of motors versus sails didn't apply to them, because they could never stop or turn in time. There are explicit rules one should read and study in navigation guides that apply to these situations. He felt a bit annoyed with the situation, but he finally realized that he should take a basic navigation course. These courses do not result in a permit but an understanding of the rules, regulations, and safety procedures. The course, approximately 10 weeks long, does not make you an expert, but it will make you more aware of what to do in different boating situations.

There was one particularly embarrassing moment when my wife and I had slept at the dock and a neighbor sailor mentioned that there was a way to silence the cables inside the mast. I told him that I had never really noticed the noise. He said that they had been particularly noisy that afternoon. I didn't understand right away, but then I remembered that my wife and I had slept in the bunk that afternoon ...*Uhh-oh!*

I didn't take too many people out on sailing adventures that year. Actually, I was more than confident; it was the others I wasn't that confident about. I was always saying, "Give it time, you're getting better. You'll be as good as anyone else pretty soon." I would say this especially on their first time out, as well as "Next time out, you won't get seasick ... hopefully!" This was my best year learning and improving my handling of a sailboat, and I considered all my experiences as part of my training.

We sailed the *Doulande* for another year, and then my brother decided to sell her. We had outgrown her as a family, and my brother thought it was time for a change. I spent the next two years in irons, or in the doldrums. I was idly standing still, reading and surfing the internet.

# 8. *Mandolin Wind*

It was between Christmas and New Year's, 1996-1997. I had just read an ad in *Boats for Sale.*

> *Mandolin Wind,* 37' Wooden Ketch
> 1976, cedar on oak frame, fiberglass deck,
> Atomic Universal Motor, Tri-axle trailer.
> Recently Surveyed. Asking $9500. Cnd. Obo.

I phoned. From that moment, I kept reading the ad and wondering about all kinds of things. It was as if a bee had stung me. I was curious, restless, anxious, hopeful, and dreaming. On January 6, I received a fax containing a copy of the boat survey and a photocopy of the boat's profile, along with a few details supplied by Mr. Vern Fairly of S.A.L.T.S., (Sailing and Life Training Society). The photocopy was horrible, but I did my best to imagine what she looked like. Following up, I called Mr. Fairly and asked him for better photocopies. He called the head office in British Columbia and had the original pictures sent down to him and then forwarded them on to me. I instantly fell off my chair when I saw them. I was drooling. I called Mr. Fairly and told him that I wanted to see the boat. An old boat she was, but a classic!

January 25, 1997

My son Marc and I left our village of St. Colomban, Quebec, around 5 am. The temperature was -28 °C (-18 °F), and we were in a blustery snowstorm that was supposed to be just about over, so said the radio. This lasted until we had passed through nearby Lachute. By the time we reached Alexandria and for the next hundred miles, we were in an ice storm. We passed at least 20 cars that had been abandoned here and there in ditches on both sides of the highway. One car was upside-down. The drivers of most of these cars had obviously lost control, by the looks of the cars' positions; although a few had just driven off to the side of the road and parked. At one point, we were driving at a speed of ten miles an hour. When we reached Kingston 5 hours later, things started to clear up. I was glad I hadn't given up driving that day, although I had come close to that decision a couple of times.

The sky became sunny with intermittent clouds, and it warmed up to -24 °C (-11 °F). That was much better. We reached Toronto by 11:30 a.m. and continued north from there to Penetanguishene, encountering a few good snow squalls on the way. We reached Penetanguishene around 1:30 p.m. and got our bearings from a lady who owned and operated a restaurant there. She naturally invited us to stay for lunch, but we declined because we wanted to have a good breakfast instead. We then proceeded to this other restaurant called the Blue Sky and ordered our breakfast. This was a treat in itself; thick back bacon along with three eggs cooked and gently laid over the bacon. There were sliced tomatoes, lettuce, roasted potatoes, toast, and coffee. Mmmm.

We prepared ourselves for the purpose of this trip and left the restaurant. Just as we arrived near the perimeter of Hindson Marina, we scanned the first few boats that came into view. There she was a real sight for sore eyes. *Mandolin Wind* was the first boat. She looked good from the highway. We felt nothing but good vibrations so far.

We had quite a time getting into the marina. Everything was locked. We managed to squirm through the gap in the main gate. We walked through snow that was two to three feet deep carrying a four foot step ladder and a camera. We were lucky because I was expecting much more. Finally we were standing in front of her. Looking at her bowsprit, I stood in amazement and wonder. My heart actually throbbed. I was in dreamland.

The next problem was getting on board. A four foot ladder was obviously no match for her; the deck was ten feet off the ground. We borrowed an eight foot ladder from another boat. With a couple of 2 x 4's that had been left on the *Mandolin Wind's* trailer, we worked out a system as best we could. We made a platform, or bridge, three feet off the ground, between the *Mandolin Wind* and the neighboring boat. Then we installed this eight foot ladder on top of this platform. A precarious situation … but finally we were on board. We were like an acrobatic act from the *Cirque du Soleil*.

Mandolin Wind Ready for her Christening after seven years

Francois making the masts parallel

Mandolin on a trial run

Rigging a temporary steering mechanism

Mandolin with her staysail and mizzen sail, perfectly balanced

Mandolin Wind with her suit of sails

It was snowing, howling, and blowing. We could feel the wind on our faces, but we were too preoccupied to feel the cold. Now with a little scrounging through the snow, which was everywhere, we uncovered three hatches. Marc climbed in through one of them while I worked on the main companionway. I finally got in. On first sight, I didn't like what I saw. There was up to three inches of frozen water on the floor inside the hull. Plus the interior was in poor shape. I was a bit saddened. The height of the inside was a bit too low; although, I could stand up straight in a couple sections of it. Overall, the interior was quite gloomy.

On the positive side, there was a bathroom door which closed upon itself, creating a small bathroom. In this position, every other section was opened up from the front to the back of the boat. In the fully open position, it closed off the back of the boat from the front and created a larger bathroom area. On the port side of the enlarged bathroom, there was a head (toilet) and a closet for wetsuits and hoods. On the starboard side, there was a high countertop with five drawers and, to its right, a cabinet door, all in one section. The countertop could be used for shaving or as a chart table for looking at navigational charts and plotting. The bathroom had two portholes, one to port and one to starboard. I could even stand up because of the skylight hatch just above.

There was another interesting thing: a forward compartment ahead of the v-berth that was used for gear storage. It contained ropes, life jackets, and fenders. There was even another compartment in front of that, which was the anchor well for the anchor rode and chain. We spent a couple of hours assessing her and then headed back to Toronto to stay overnight at my sister's.

After we left the marina, I was speechless for the next two to three hours. Not until the next day did I again start to talk about the *Mandolin Wind*. It had all started to sink in and make some kind of sense. I now felt that she could provide my family and me with many hours of enjoyment. I began to feel this warmth, this intrigue, grow slowly inside of me. My trip had not been in vain.

The next day we left for Brantford, Ontario, to look at another boat, a steel 28' Glen-L model. It was less interesting. We had taken pictures of the two boats. By noon that Sunday we were back on our way to St. Colomban, which we reached at around 8:30 p.m.

January 28th, 1997

In the week that followed, I made an offer to Mr. Fairly based on the resale value of the *Mandolin Wind,* arrived at by calculating what it would fetch if it had to be dismantled and sold for parts. I was nervous when I made the offer and Mr. Fairly was a bit reluctant. He asked me to wait 24-48 hours for an answer. January 29th my offer was accepted. I had harped on the fact that there was too much ice in the hull, and I think that this could have been the deciding factor. Actually, the boat was too far away for them to verify this, and time was on my side. The ice had not damaged the hull. It had frozen and expanded in the upward direction.

February 5th, 1997

With a credit margin approved by the bank, I was ready to have the deal closed. This took place at Tim Horton's donut shop in Hawkesbury, Ontario; and after all that, she was mine. I drove back home floating on cloud nine. This boat was like a drug. It was seductive, mesmerizing, and captivating; even my son Marc felt this way. I had reached my ultimate goal by acquiring possession of this beautiful sailing vessel. What a great feeling.

Mr. Fairly from S.A.L.T.S. believed that I had made a good purchase and that she was an eye catcher. A new adventure was about to begin if my health permitted. This boat had style and character. She was green on the top sides with copper bottom paint below the water line. Her deck and cabin were all white with mahogany, cedar and some teak trim. Her two masts and booms were painted white as well.

The boat-show came around and I purchased a wheel helm made of mahogany, which would replace the regular tiller. I also purchased a navy blue T-shirt with a maroon polo collar and my boat's name embroidered in maroon on the left breast. I was informed that it would cost $120 for a six day pass to go through the Trent-Severn Waterway plus $30 extra per day, plus $20 each for the Iroquois Locks and the Eisenhower Locks; maybe more because I exceeded the thirty foot regulation by six inches (they didn't charge for the three foot boomkin and the four foot bowsprit). I also met a machinist who could custom make me a nine inch tiller of cast iron to adapt to my rudder post. This would be needed to convert the tiller (steering bar) to a wheel helm by way of cables.

I talked to a Nova Scotian from Marin Traders in Digby, Nova Scotia. This person was really an Acadian and what a special accent he had when he talked French. In a way it is like comparing the north and south in certain parts of the states. He would be able to supply me with all the hardware I might need brass or galvanized. Then there was bottom paint from another company called Matchless Paints in Dartmouth, N.S. One gallon of fisherman's red bottom paint would only cost me $50, including delivery. The paint itself was around $29. Still, one gallon of copper bottom paint costs $120 here in Quebec. Vern Fairly had 8 mahogany pins for sale. These were good for tying down the halyards and so forth, and they would give the boat a salty look.

February 10th, 1997

I went and saw a chap about having modifications done on *Mandolin's* trailer. He said that he would be able to give me a better estimate once I brought him the trailer, especially since I needed a steel cradle and modifications to the frame. In the meantime, he thought it wiser to motor the boat down the Trent-Severn Waterway. It would be easier on the boat, and the trip would be wonderful, so picturesque and educational at the same time. He offered to lend me the marine charts for the trip right up to Kingston.

I was having a hard time sitting still. The boat was so far away and I found it hard not to be able to do something; anything. I found a part-time job on Saturdays mornings for the next 10 weeks. I made $60 a shot. This would pay paid part of my traveling expenses to the boat to prepare it for its trip to its new home in the spring.

March 9th, 1997

I phoned Mr. D. Haron, the previous owner, who had donated the boat to S.A.L.T.S. It was supposed to have a plough anchor on board; however, this was missing. This was my first deception of many to come. I made arrangements by telephone with his wife Betty for her to purchase and have a tarp installed on the boat. I had sent them money for this but it never got done. Her husband had purchased the tarp, but he had never bothered to put it on and I never got to see it. Deceptions come in all shapes and sizes. He mentioned of some pictures which he would mail to me, and he thought that it would also be a better idea to have the boat hauled. He had a balance of C1311 Copper bottom paint, probably enough for this coming year.

Mr. Haron mentioned that if there were any problems with the motor, it would be with the starter. Therefore, without hesitation, I had the starter rebuilt. As for the motor itself, it was supposed to have been rebuilt a few years earlier. The mizzenmast boom was also fairly new. The hull seemed sound.

March 11th, 1997

I received the pictures of *Mandolin Wind* with her sails up. What a nice boat she was. I was proud, happy, and relieved. I had dreamed that the boat was beautiful, and beautiful she was. I hoped to live long enough to enjoy her. I wanted to share my happiness and joy with everyone. I went out and had enlargements made of the pictures. Six of them I put in my home and one of them I used like a calendar at the office. My daughter put a framed one in her apartment.

March 18th, 1997

A friend offered his time to come with me to Penetanguishene. We would take the measurements of the trailer and the boat so as to be able to build a steel cradle and also do a better analysis of the boat. I relied a lot on his expertise as an engineer and as a sailor. I also brought back as many boat items as possible in the van. My wife and I wanted to spend our two-week long holiday in May, boating back by motor to its new home.

Information was starting to trickle in from the Internet. This was a practical source for good, sound information. Might I say it was also interesting and fun!

# 9. Renovation, Part One

April 22nd, 1997

*Mandolin Wind* started her trip to her new home. She was gently loaded onto a 48-foot flatbed trailer with her trailer also placed piggyback on the same flatbed trailer. It cost $1,000. to have it hauled back. It was the safest bet and worth every penny. She was hauled in the wee hours of the morning on a 7½ hour ride from Penetanguishene, Ontario, to Oka, Quebec, some four hundred miles away. We were insured and stress-free.

A funny thing happened that morning; my sister was on her way back from a meeting in Orillia, just north of Toronto. She was driving on Hwy. 400 with a friend who asked, "What is that on the road ahead? It's awfully big, like a house or something."

Then, as they approached the object, my sister said, "That looks like the boat my brother just bought." Then when she got close enough, she read the name on the transom, *Mandolin Wind*. "Yes, that's his boat, alright!" Her friend didn't believe her, and even my sister couldn't swear by it because it had been some three months since she had seen the photos. What a coincidence for her to be on that stretch of road at the same moment that my boat was being hauled.

Once in Oka, the boat would be cradled in the yard. She would have to wait to get a facelift. I was told by Can Am, the trucking company that she would arrive around 2:00 p.m. on Wednesday the 23rd. A good deal of her equipment was already in Quebec. I was anxious, happy, and worried all at the same time. Would everything go well? I was sure that it would. Well, finally the boat arrived in Oka. Welcome home, *Mandolin Wind!*

April 24th, 1997

Now that I was able to see her better, I was beginning to let reality sink in. There was a lot to do to make the boat right; so much that I was getting a little worried. Did I have enough time to make her floatable by the end of May? Did I have enough money? Would my health hold out? Did I have the drive? Well, there was only one way to find out. I was determined to make my dream come true. I'd already seen what I could do with one sailboat that I had refurbished, so imagine what I could do with a whole ship! I knew that my family wouldn't let me down either. Everyone said I was courageous; that meant I was nuts! No one believed in what I wanted to do. It wasn't worth the effort. My having this project as a hobby or pastime was great, but almost everyone seemed to be pessimistic about it going as planned. They were probably right.

When I purchased the *Mandolin Wind*, I was lacking in experience and quite short on confidence. What I did to compensate for these shortcomings was to do research and always write down every thought I had on the subject; this included likely candidates for informing me on any given matter. Every thought was important, even the stupid ones. When you're new at this game, you need as much information as possible.

My biggest asset was the Internet. I started using the Internet quite a bit that year, and I learned a lot. I found all kinds of answers to questions such as the following. When replacing a board on the hull, how much tolerance, or gap, is required for expansion? I created a real collection of information on every subject from varnishes, to spars, to sails, to motors. I navigated between at least 50 different websites such as *Wooden Boats* magazine, *Sail* magazine, boat restorers, and so on. I spent approximately three hours per day, or 10-18 hours per week, searching, reading, printing, and cruising books, weather forecasts and boats for sale. I kept finding new leads. I learned a lot about sailing and boats this way as well.

People that are well-informed about wooden boats today are not as common as you would think. You can accumulate information from magazine articles, you can read books, you can talk to workers at marine supply stores ... but the best prospects are other owners or past owners of wooden boats. Then there are the boat shows where the marine supply companies show their wares. Some come from faraway places. At the Montréal Boat Show, there was The Marine Traders Company from Nova Scotia. They gave me a few important leads and helped me out a lot.

April 25th, 1997

I telephoned Mr. Fairly and he gave me the name of a marine supply store in Ottawa called The Chandlery. Mr. Fairly recommended Sikaflex, a polysulfide sealant, or a construction type polyurethane to seal the joints. I also talked to Mr. Huberto, a master electrician, and negotiated a deal with him for his services as an electrician and as a mechanic.

One day, my engineering friend and I were talking about adapting a wheel helm to the boat, but in a different way than we had first planned. We would make a steering box with a worm and spur gear. He mentioned that he would come down to the boat on Sunday, and that he also had a surprise for me. He invited me over to his house. Once there, he told me that he had finished a project and asked me to open this huge box. Inside, there was this awfully heavy piece; it was an anchor, handmade by him for my boat. It was identical to a 35-pound Bruce anchor. It was unbelievable! He had made this himself. It was to replace the one that had gotten away. I didn't know what to say, I was so happy and extremely grateful.

I called various places for prices on the silicone caulking, and the prices ranged from $11.95 to $16.95 a tube. With 32 tubes to buy, this wouldn't be cheap. Mr. Fairly had mentioned using a bent file tail to clean out the seams on the boat. I finally decided on a Formica cutter, with the tip ground flat.

I had three weekends to work on the boat plus a 17-day holiday. I also had some free evenings to advance the work on boat parts at the house. I believed I would have enough time to prepare the boat for the season. I made a support on the side of the shed to hold my two booms horizontally. I also refinished the drawer surfaces and the tiller with a bright marine varnish. Boy, they were beautiful! Only three more doors to do and a whole boat to boot. I brought home all the woodwork possible to sand and varnish during the evenings.

April 26th & 27th, 1997

Friday night I loaded up my Plymouth Colt van. This little van was very practical for its economical usage, its size, and the way it could house all my tools behind the back seat and still carry five passengers. That Saturday, Marc and I went down to the boat. He was a last year high school student. He was very smart and he looked like Brad Pitt. He worked hard all day. I was surprised by his enthusiasm and quite happy to have him there helping me. I was feeling cheerful. He removed all the portholes, handrails, moldings, air traps, hatches, and some of the rigging. On top of that, he scrapped and sanded the exterior of the cabin. It took him two whole days. The next weekend, he patched the cabin with fiberglass and painted it. With all the headway we were making, it looked promising. I decided to pay Marc for the time he spent helping me, seeing that he didn't have a summer job. I proposed $25 per day to keep his motivation alive, and this suited him well and I had a friend.

Jacinthe came with us the next Sunday, and she also impressed me. She removed all the interior doors and the back of a bench. She removed a few other items, and then she spent the rest of the afternoon sanding the interior. She was starting to show interest in *Mandolin Wind*. She was starting to like the boat. As for myself, I made a long ladder that was a bit on the heavy side but strong and sturdy. I scrapped out the hull seams for two full days. This represented 1/6 of the work that needed to be done on the hull alone. This was really hard work and my arms felt as if there were cement blocks tied to them. As the days wore on, my arms got stronger.

I really liked the interior layout of the boat. It was truly special. It was originally constructed to sleep one, although it could easily sleep three. The last owner had increased the size of the motor and had changed its position in regards to the propeller shaft. This project had created a disaster area. The kitchen had been completely destroyed to make room for this change, so I planned on rebuilding new cabinets. More work…

I hadn't been this happy since I had got married both times, in 1964 and 1974. I am very grateful to Jacinthe for allowing me this new adventure that I am experiencing. I got very tired from all the work, but so what? One day, after working on the boat, I even found the time at home to replace an outdoor spigot. I also hung up a painting, helped Roxanne with her English, and reconfigured the printer for the computer. I washed the dishes and washed the wheels of my van while Frank washed the rest of it. It was 10:20 pm when I headed off to bed. I adored my boat.

May 3rd, 1997

That morning was cold and grey. It started raining around 11:00 a.m. Jacinthe and I were on our way to the Chandlery in Ottawa. My goal was to obtain information on wooden boat restoration that could be of help to me. I finally found a book written by the West System Company, and it had some good ideas for restoring certain structures of the boat. I was quite satisfied with it. Not only that, I got the names of two people who repaired and built wooden boats in the vicinity. They were both located on Rideau Canal.

Once home that evening, I instantly called Mr. Porter. I explained what I had in mind in regards to the boat. I had lost a day's work, but I had regained it by obtaining valuable information which would save me precious time. Mr. Porter mentioned that I should only use Sikaflex to fill the seams I had cleaned out, and that I shouldn't use it on any of the other seams that were good. This was good advice. Something told me I should have listened to him. However, because of my over zealous concern for safety, I didn't. Another important piece of advice he gave me was to always repair wooden areas with wood, not epoxy or fillers. This made sense, and I followed this advice, amazingly. Sometimes I listen.

May 4th, 1997

Marc got a summer job at some french fry stand, and I started working on the boat alone. I was happy for him, even though I had lost my favorite helper. This boat would have given Marc an understanding of woodworking, fiberglass, electricity, and mechanics, plus in many other areas. However, this other choice was important to him as well. His first steps toward eventual independence.

It was blowing hard, and it was cold enough for me to have to wear a shirt, sweatshirt, and a winter jacket. I finished scraping out the seams, 32 of them below the water line, not counting the ones in the solid keel. I also removed the two foot stainless steel whisker underneath the bowsprit. Its primary purpose was to keep the mast under tension. I was going to have it modified by my "anchor making" friend. I also did the calculations for my wheel helm. My rudder was offset 1 1/2" to the left, and with the 2 5/8" offset of the worm gear and spur gear to the right, the wheel helm would be off center only 1 1/8". The length of the shaft for the wheel would need to be only 14" long. This would work fine. I painted two coats of white on the outside of the two air intake scoops (with the inside of them painted forest green), which I had sandblasted earlier. I had worked from 9:30 a.m. until 4:30 p.m. and I was bushed.

May 12th, 1997

It rained intermittently most of the day, so I decided to clean the motor and the bilge. I also removed the starter to have it repaired. I saw another wooden boat, a cutter (a converted schooner), made in Nova Scotia. She was an older boat than mine, a little narrower and about the same length. I thought that maybe this boat owner and I could compare notes.

That Sunday I stayed home and sanded all day, outside the shed. It was windy with lots of sunshine, but cool. I called Jamestown the next day to order the cotton bails that I needed for the boat seams. I had ordered my Sikaflex from Oka Marina. They gave me a fair price and they agreed to take back what I didn't use. I changed my mind about using Sikaflex to repair the boat. I decided to clean and fill the seams with cotton before applying the Sikaflex to the whole ship, just to be on the safe side. Later on in the fall, I saw that Mr. Porter had been right on the money. Apparently, the rest of the seams were good. Too bad I hadn't followed his advice. I would have saved myself at least seven to ten days' work and money as well. My vacation was to start on the 17th of May.

May 14, 1997

I was ready to face the task, the big boat. I had applied a second coat of varnish to all my doors. One more coat left to do. The starter was rebuilt at a cost of $60. It got new bearings, solenoid brushes, and a newly turned armature. My caulking cotton and the Sikaflex 240 were reserved. I found an interesting internet site on wooden boats which were made in Camden, Maine. I also talked to a boat builder, Mr. Low, who had an 8,000-square-foot building and a travel lift to haul boats out of the Rideau Canal.

During my vacation, I worked regularly from 8:30 a.m. to 5:00 p.m. every single day. Believe me, when the evenings rolled around, I was dead exhausted. I lost 7 1/2 pounds. I was starting to get into shape. I filled the seams with cotton, then with Sikaflex, and sanded the hull. Then I repaired any gouges and uncovered bolt holes with wood. I finished it all off with C1311 Copper bottom paint, the leftover paint that Betty had given me. Boy was the boat starting to look like new. I proceeded to paint the topsides with two coats of Armor Coat forest green enamel. Then I continued painting a five and one half inch wide, Chinese red boot stripe and varnished the two inch side moldings which were three inches below the deck line on the top side. Jacinthe and I also varnished the bowsprit.

Now my vacation was over and I was back on my regular job, but my work on the boat wasn't finished. Actually, I was really discouraged for a day or so, but then my wife gave me a few words of encouragement. My son, Francois, also encouraged me by coming down to the boat to help me caulk it. On another occasion, he helped sand one side of the hull. Believe me, the latter was the worst. That really motivated me. He came and helped on three different occasions, and I really appreciated it.

I was doing this for myself. Those seventeen days of vacation were hard, and I mean hard, for I had to rely on my own energy. I really liked the experience, but once will be enough. This kind of work was suited for younger men. I'd learned a lot and I had also made many friends. There was always someone there to chat with a bit. I was lucky in one way; I had good weather to work on the boat. It was never too hot or too cold. It was just right. I couldn't explain it, but this period of my life was very important to me. It seemed like this was what I had always wanted to do.

June 22, 1997

The 22nd of June was the official day to put the boat into the water. When I got to Oka around 2:00 p.m., the boat was already being lowered into the water. *Mandolin Wind* appeared very smart and distinguished. During the next week, until June 30th, I prepared the boat for her trip to Valleyfield, her new home. I laid the two masts down on two wooden saw horses, along with two center supports. Then the masts were lashed down at each end of the boat. There were many things that were unfinished. I had only begun to prepare the essentials.

On the 29th of June, I took the boat out for a test run. I let the motor run for half an hour and then I asked a marina dockhand if he would come along for a trial run of the boat. I had very little room to pull out of the docking space, and I had no experience with a boat of this size. She seemed enormous. I noticed that the engine ran a bit hot. When we came back to the dock, I was very nervous. An onlooker, the owner of the wooden cutter, took a couple of pictures as I passed by the docks. Everything went well, even when it came time to pull up to the dock. I had to make a 180-degree turn on a dime to position the sailboat alongside the dock. There were boats on all sides. Yes, I did it in one attempt like a pro, but, boy was the boat long with its boomkin and bowsprit!

# 10. Oka to Valleyfield

Jacinthe gave my deckhand and me a ride to Oka. Jacinthe was scheduled to work at St-Benoit Hospital that day, and the dock at Oka was only 10 minutes away. She dropped off her sister, Robin, and me around 6:30 a.m. At 6:45 a.m., Robin and I cast off for our trip to Valleyfield. Robin was my designated deckhand for the day. She was my favorite sister-in-law. She was a tiny, black haired person with a fun personality, always ready to give a hand. Today she was inexperienced, and on top of that, she seemed really hungover from partying the night before. She'd had next to no sleep, and by the smell of the fumes coming from her, I was going to be in for quite a day.

We departed Oka with a clear sky and a cool breeze of 5 to 10 knots on our heels. I had complete self confidence because of my experience making the trip five years earlier. With a shove on the front of the boat given by a stranger on hand and with my captain's talents, I got the boat out of its tight spot with forward and reverse motions. *Bravo!* I was proud of myself. That was pretty good for someone who didn't really know this boat yet.

After 20 minutes on the lake, I was panicking. The motor was about to bust or something. I shut it down and instructed my deckhand to keep her eyes open for any signs of danger on the horizon. I checked the oil level and the state of the engine. Everything seemed fine. I started the motor again. The motor was very noisy, not a knocking noise just noisy and the temperature kept steady around 220 degrees F. at all times. A marine motor uses fresh or salt water directly, and so it didn't have time to boil or build up a head of steam. I finally got the motor temperature down to around 200 to 210 degrees F. by reducing my r.p.m. a bit.

There were two foot waves, and so far, the trip was very pleasant. Rob had retired to lie down on the forward deck, face down. I was approaching some buoys, but I couldn't identify them by their colors or their numbers. The sun was low on the horizon, and the buoys were between me and the sun. I also didn't have my binoculars. *Merde (shit)!* I ended up passing the buoy on the wrong side. It was a red one. *Encore merde!* I turned around and backtracked, hoping not to hit anything. It wasn't like me to leave my charts inside the boat and not look at them. Everything worked out all right though. There was no imminent danger, so I continued on.

Twenty minutes later I was approaching the Metropolitan Bridge, which is in between the Lake of Two Mountains and Lake St-Louis. Again two unidentifiable buoys, one red and one green. Why were the buoys reversed in their locations? It seemed to me that they were positioned in the opposite order to that of the other buoys. This was strange. Well, I just did the contrary what I had done with the other two buoys. I was sure I was right. I asked Rob to go and fetch the charts. Again, I had made a navigational error. I was coming through the buoys in the wrong direction. There was a shallow area some two to three hundred feet from the red buoy. It was too late now, so I continued on my way but very, very slowly.

I didn't have a depth sounder, and I didn't have time to show my shipmate how to check the depth. Like a bat flying in a glass gift shop, I made it through without a hitch. We were one foot higher above the chart level, and this is what saved us. Finally we arrived at Ste. Anne de Bellevue. The lock gates were open, so we motored on into the interior and tied up along the wall and paid the $20.50 to pass through the lock. We were lowered twelve inches. What an experience for my newborn shipmate! She managed to stay aboard the boat. *Wonderful!* We were making progress. After passing through the lock, we tied up along the dock dead center of the town of Ste. Anne de Bellevue. It was a most beautiful place.

Rob went to buy us (her especially) some coffee. I told her where to go and "Please don't run; you might just kill yourself!" I took out my golfing umbrella to protect myself from the now hot sun and rested as I waited for Rob. There I was, sitting on my dumpy boat, the masts just lying there on their sides, the unfinished cabin in a patched state. She looked like some kind of Chinese junk, especially with my red, white, and blue golfing umbrella. What a sight!

Finally, Rob came back … empty-handed. It had taken some time for her to make the hundred yards walk to the lock, cross the lock, and then walk another hundred yards to get to me. In all this excitement, I dropped the gaff pole in the water, and it took me ten minutes to fish it out. Good thing it floated. The trick was to lay a rope across the pole and try to slowly drag it back to the boat. Rob didn't find any coffee because she couldn't find any restaurants that were open. I explained to her that if she walked over to the taxi stand and asked, they would tell her where to go. Twenty minutes later, guess who arrived with the coffee? Party time!

The newborn sailor wanted to learn how to tie up a boat to a dock. "Okay, come with me onto the dock," I told her. We got down on our knees in front of the dock cleat and put our precious coffees down next to us. I took the line and showed her how to make a half hitch knot. "Okay Rob." It was her turn. Her knot wasn't right! No problem. I showed her again. "Do it like this, okay?" What? It was wrong again? "Here," I said, "give me the rope!" I tied the knot again … oops! I spilled my coffee. I grumbled to myself. I kept my calm and gave her a big smile. It didn't matter. She tried again, but to no avail. I went to Rob's other side and began to show her again, and "pop"! There went Rob's coffee. Okay, that's enough for this morning and so we started up again and continued on our journey.

I made use of the marine charts to get us through Lake St-Louis. We passed through a canal like channel, and then we passed Windmill Point. Three power boats were approaching us rapidly. Two of them were making fairly big waves, which were strong enough to shake the two masts on the deck. I thought they were going to fall overboard. When the third boat approached, I turned my boat towards him as if I was trying to ram him. He understood and pulled away from me. I retied my masts to the ship more securely.

Finally we arrived at the Beauharnois Locks. The locks were gigantic. What a sight! We went to one side of these locks, where there was a small dock to which four or five small boats could be tied up at a time. I backed her into place, but not without putting a nice scratch on the newly painted hull. That annoyed me considerably, especially when I thought of how many hours of work had gone into the boat.

After settling my frayed nerves, I climbed the steps to get to a phone that rang through to the lock master. I gave him all the basic information, such as the name of the boat, the size of the boat, and the registration information. Then I returned to my boat and waited for further instructions. There was a gigantic electronic panel that relayed back instructions. They had mentioned on the phone that there would be approximately a half-hour wait. With that in mind, and it being 11:45 a.m., I suggested to Rob that we eat lunch. Once we got going, it would be an hour or more before we got another chance. So tomato sandwiches it was. With my first bite, there was a PA message telling us to get ready, that we were about to be let into the locks, so much for lunch. Then the big gates opened up.

It never ceases to impress me, the size of these locks. They gave us the green light, and in we went. I had this really weird sensation as I heard the water still running in between the granite walls and dripping. This sound echoed and was amplified, along with any noise that we made. It was both awesome and spooky. Now I knew what it felt like to be a dwarf in a fairy tale. We tied up along the granite type block walls in the front of the first lock. There were two ropes dangling, waiting for us to tie them to our forward and aft cleats. I explained to Robin the importance of keeping the boat in a tight position with the wall as the lock master lets in the water. As the water came in from beneath us, it created all kinds of undercurrents; and this drew the boat away from the wall. Still we managed to keep the boat close to the wall with success. We passed through two locks, and we were lifted some ninety feet. Amazing!

The next sixteen miles we would travel through the Beauharnois Canal on our way to Lake St-Francis. This is a major seaway canal and the ships can reach as much as seven hundred and forty feet long. The canal is around four hundred feet wide with a current of about two knots, which we had to motor against. There was also a fairly good headwind of ten knots and a very hot sun. This made the motor run continually at 220 degrees F. and this I didn't like. I just hoped that she (the engine) would hold out. It was a good thing that the engine ran continually on fresh water, or it would have overheated. There was no way of getting help, except to tie up somewhere and walk back to the locks or ahead to some unknown place. My deckhand returned for a little nap under the two masts at the fo'c'sle, so as not to have the sun in her eyes.

The canal was indeed not picturesque, and the time passed by ever so slowly with a very hot sun to boot. We passed under two vertical lift bridges, and finally we arrived at the mouth of the canal. The waves increased to a two foot height, caused by the three to four mile fetch that the wind had, coming across the lake towards us. The lake was a great sight. The time was 3:45 p.m. We followed one set of buoys (green on the left) as though we were returning from the sea and then followed the channel buoys into the Valleyfield Marina, again using the same rule (red, right returning). With the motor smoking and at a temperature of 220 degrees F. and a hungover sailor, we made it to our dock, where we slipped in between an Alberg 30 and a Tanzer 29. There were two men there who gave us assistance tying up. We finished tying up at 4:15 p.m. Thank you, God, no hitches.

Jacinthe was there. She had been waiting for about an hour. She had gone to see the coastguard because we were an hour and fifteen minutes late. They weren't worried for the moment. Jacinthe came back to the dock. When she saw us, she had a nice big smile on. The three of us stood around and talked for a while, and then we started to prepare to leave the boat. It turned out to be a very nice day. I had expected a lot out of Robin, and she had delivered.

The boat was finally in Valleyfield, six months after I had purchased her. The hull was in perfect shape. She looked serene. Phase two of her initial renovation was coming up. There was the cabin to finish and the two masts to paint and install. There might be two, maybe three weekends of work for the cabin, and then the masts. By the 1st of August, the boat would hopefully be ready for sailing. It would not be before then, because that day I found an area of rot in the mainmast and another one in the mizzenmast that had to be repaired.

There was so much to do, and every job took a lot of time; much more than I had expected. I was discouraged at not being able to sail the boat any sooner, but I still loved doing what I was doing. I'd be better prepared next spring. I had a Canadian flag placed on *Mandolin's* backstay. I would have liked to spend the First of July (Canada Day) with *Mandolin Wind,* but I couldn't. Oh well, happy Canada Day!

# 11. A Mast-ive Refit

August 6th, 1997

I used up the next five weekends repairing, sanding, and painting the two masts. On the foremast, I removed a rot spot 1½ inches wide by 1½ inches deep by forty eight inches long on one of the edges of the mast. Then I removed one that was six inches wide by 1½ inches deep by eighteen inches long on the mizzenmast. On the mizzenmast, I made two cuts at a forty-five degree angle (like a green bean cut). This was a major operation because one-third of the thickness of the stock was being removed. I used kiln dried spruce on the mainmast and air dried spruce on the mizzen. Both operations turned out to be a success. I removed the seventeen shrouds and had them sandblasted, and then I painted them at home, applying a number of splashes of aluminum paint onto the white siding of my house. No one could have done a better job.

I used wood and glue and some epoxy for the repairs to the masts. I painted them with white Armor Coat and reinstalled the seventeen shrouds. I worked seven days out of ten, having lost three days due to rain. I was proud of my accomplishments. My daughter gave me a good hand as well, sanding the masts. Now this was very impressive to me, seeing a person like her do this work. She was studying for a bachelor's degree in piano interpretation. Today she has a Master's degree in the same field and a second bachelors degree in music education for primary school and high school. She was a tiny person and had her mother's bubbly character and always smiling. I enjoyed her company very much and we enjoyed sharing our days working and just being around other boats in the marina ambiance.

It took one day to install the masts with the help of my oldest son, Francois, and my wife. It was relatively easy until we got close to the end. There were signs of a thunderstorm, and Francois was forty feet up at the top of the steel crane next to the mast top trying to install a turnbuckle and cable. The turnbuckle would secure the cable (which was already attached to the mizzenmast) to the mainmast. Motorboats kept passing by and making waves, causing the top of the mast to sway four to five feet at times. Finally Francois managed by holding the mast still with one hand and then letting go, and with a flurry of movements, finally stuck the securing pin into the turnbuckle that was attached to the cable. Now the two masts were attached to each other by the ten foot cable and a turnbuckle, which was there to make the final adjustments so that the masts were perfectly parallel to each another.

The next challenge for him was to install the circular locking pin through the turnbuckle's securing pin, which would prevent the turnbuckle from slipping out and letting the mizzen mast fall. Done! The last challenge: the crane's hoisting cable wouldn't release from the mast. The lightning flashes were very close now, only some twenty five hundred to five thousand feet away. After a few more attempts, Francois finally got the cable free and rambled down the crane as I stored the hook, cable, and boom.

It started to pour, and there were flashes of lightning. All three of us went inside the boat. We were soaked, but the job was done. It was going on 6 p.m. and my son wanted to leave to join his friends. There was an odor of gas probably caused by the ketch behind us, so I advised Jacinthe and Francois not to smoke. Once the storm passed over, we left the fuel dock where the crane was and headed back to our own dock. Francois and Jacinthe both left, and once everything was secured, so did I. I still smelled gas from the other boat as I left for home.

The next day my wife and I returned to the boat, and as I opened the hatch, there was still a smell of gas lingering. There was also gas floating on the water all around the exterior of the boat. It was then that I realized that it was coming from my boat. Again, I advised Jacinthe not to smoke and to stay on the dock while I removed the engine compartment cover to look for the source of the trouble. First off, two inches of water had accumulated in the boat; that meant my bilge pump had stopped working. It couldn't have been for more than a few hours. Normally the pump ran for about 30-60 seconds every 30-45 minutes. It turned out to be the float switch that was defective. I then turned my attention to the gas leak. It was coming from a split in the rubber hose that was fastened to the gas line filter.

Mr. MacSween, the marina manager came over and told my wife that the neighbors were complaining about a gas leak, and that they thought it was coming from our boat. After I explained the situation to Mr. MacSween, he asked me to get a bottle of dishwashing soap. He showed me how, by placing a couple of drops here and there on the water, it actually chased away the gas. His idea worked great.

We were more than lucky. First of all, my wife and son both smoked. What had saved us that day and the day before was my having forbidden the two of them to smoke. Further, on this particular day, I was the one who first opened the hatch, rather than my wife. If she had been the first to arrive, she could have just lit up a cigarette while waiting for me. The third stroke of luck was that my electric pump had quit because of a faulty switch. This switch had been repaired with some type of epoxy or sealant which the gas had most likely eaten away. The water had entered and jammed the micro switch in the off position, preventing a possible spark which could have had serious consequences.

It took another two days to set the forestay, backstay, and upper, middle, and lower shrouds, forward and aft. There were seventeen of them. I had help from my Alberg neighbor in tensioning the shrouds and stays. This guy, a wiry six footer and sixty-six years old, was a perfect replica of Jacques Cousteau right down to the tuque (wool cap), the funny small beard, and Parisian accent.

I had help from another sailor that afternoon with the extension on the roller reefer. I found that my masts had too much rake (they were leaning too far backwards), so I shortened the distance between the bottom of the roller reefer and the deck fitting by 1½ inches. This permitted my two masts to lean forward some four to five inches. I had planned to put on all my sails that day, but all I had time for was installing the genoa onto the roller reefer. The tension on the cables wasn't quite right, so I added that task to my work calendar. I would get to it the next Saturday when my boys would come help out. Come hell or high water, those sails were going up, and I was going sailing!

# 12. *Mandolin Wind's* First Sail

I came to understand why *Mandolin Wind* was so named. Her hull was made of wood and round like a mandolin's body, and her masts were the necks of the instrument. Her stays and shrouds were her strings, and the wind was the hand that strummed her strings. What a fitting name for such a boat. It captured her essence.

August 13th, 1997

On Saturday, Marc, Francois, and I brought out *Mandolin's* suit of clothes. This was to be her first time wearing them after two years on dry dock. It took all day, but the three sails were finally on, along with the white sail covers. The sail on the mizzen had got snagged at the spreader level. I saved that problem for the following day. At 5:00 p.m. I instructed Francois and Marc to get us some hot dogs, fries, and pop. I'm sure Francois was more than happy to drive my van and Marc as well, just to get a break ... teenagers. I fixed the mizzen sail as best I could for the time being. When they got back, we untied the boat and headed out onto the lake, eating as we motored along.

Marc and Francois prepared the mainsail as I proudly watched them. Dressed in their beige shorts, T-shirts, running shoes, and baseball caps, they looked like a professional sailing team. They hoisted up the mainsail and pulled in the sheets to flatten it. They heaved the genoa sheets and pulled the genoa out of its rolled form and fully extended it, then flattened it. The mizzen sail stayed put because of its slight tracking problem that we would correct the next day. Once the mainsail and the genoa were up, we were awed by their sizes and shapes. *Mandolin Wind* moved along gracefully and as smoothly as skis gliding on new snow. She had this special interaction with the waves. It was as if the waves would come up against the hull and try to lift the boat, but the boat wouldn't react right away; and when the waves receded from the hull, the boat would react just as fast as the wave. It was a less rocking affair compared to the *Doulande,* the twenty two foot Tanzer.

My sons and I were all wearing big smiles. I walked on the deck to the front of the boat. Marc gave me the time, 7:00 p.m. One half hour and we would have to head back so we would have enough time to tie up the boat before nightfall. The sun was disappearing on the horizon, and the wind had dropped to three to five knots. The winch on the foremast worked perfectly, and so did the roller furler with the genoa. We got back to the dock where our neighbors greeted us with camera in hand. That was a proud moment for us. Everyone thought the boat looked salty in the sunset.

I sent Francois out for a six-pack to celebrate our feat. My dock neighbors joined us. The air was nice and warm that evening. Inside me, I was rushing, my mind computing everything and my heart expanding to its limit. I'm glad that my sons were there with me (and my neighbors also) to share this moment by being a good pair of friendly ears. I had a hard time wiping the grin off my face. I went to sleep that night wearing a smile. Later, my neighbor gave me two pictures that showed us coming in towards the dock that evening. I really appreciated the gesture.

August 14th, 1997

I continued to install pieces on the boat, such as a radar reflector, two other flags, a compass, wiring for the navigation lights, and the V.H.F. There were three corrections that I had to make to the sails. The first was to the genoa. It was too loose and sloppy; we couldn't apply enough tension to flatten it properly, and it needed a U.V. protection cover made of the forest green Sumbrella material. The second correction was to the mainsail. It had to be shortened by six inches. It had never been adjusted and again I couldn't fully flatten it out. This also let my boom down much too low. The third correction was to clean the epoxy from the track midway up the mizzen, which in turn would permit the sail on this mast to be hoisted completely to the top. This was a job for Marc; he would need to climb up the mast to get the chore done. This was always a frightful part of being a sailor, climbing the masts. The job went without a hitch. The boat was looking smarter and smarter as the work progressed. She looked better by the day.

But then bad luck again resurfaced. My bilge pump quit on me again. The problem arose after I washed down all the inside bilges and ran the pump to remove the gas and water mixture. When the water level in the bilge rose, the bilge pump started up and sucked out the water. This caused the movement of floating debris towards the pump, which obstructed the impeller, and in turn burned up the motor. I had one inch of water above my floorboards. I reinstalled the backup pump (the original pump) and finished the job.

August 22/23rd, 1997

Roxanne had waited seven months for a chance to come sailing with *Mandolin Wind*. She had worked on the two masts, scraping and sanding them, as well as other projects on the boat. The wind was at 12 knots (force two) fresh from the west by northwest. There was a little more than the occasional white caps here and there. We sailed for seven hours. The slow, bobbing movement of the boat as it gracefully tacked from one side to the other felt wonderful. It took on three foot waves as if they were mere ripples. I found the tiller was a bit stiff when all three sails were up in this strength of wind, and the boat heeled to a fifteen-degree angle. If it had blowed any harder, I would have lowered the mizzen sail. Inside the boat, I felt a bit crowded during the sailing trek. I was more at ease outside. Though my boat seemed very solid, once back at the marina, I discovered that it was taking on more water. The pump was running every ten minutes instead of the usual forty five minutes. The problem, which lasted about twelve hours, was due to the fact that the hull works while sailing. Apparently, all planked hulls do this. As the season progressed, this problem became less evident as the planks swelled up tighter.

August 29/30th, 1997

I continued to adjust the stays and shrouds. I shortened the length of the roller furler another ½ inch. For a second time, I adjusted all my stays and shrouds. It takes the better part of a day to do this at least twice. That Sunday, I took Jacinthe and my brother out for their first sail on *Mandolin Wind*. The winds were around force two (ten knots) with the occasional white caps. We sailed for five glorious hours, and naturally we again had the most agreeable time that you could possibly have on a sailboat. The boat handled so well. She was just as good as the Tanzer tacking upwind.

*Mandolin Wind* seemed to be slower than other boats her size, but apparently not so according to some other people who had seen her perform. This was to be tested further. In mild winds, with her heavy hull, lighter thirty footers could outmaneuver her. I was confident that in strong winds (force 3-4), she would fare quite well. Now when the bigger motor cruisers passed by me, they didn't worry me; the boat responded well to their wakes. It was a lot of fun walking about on the spacious deck. This sailing machine pleased me more and more every day.

I removed the motor thermostat to see if it would have an effect on the heat generated by the motor. Well, not at all. Next, I went and bought white spaghettis for the shrouds and planned on installing them the following season. I bought two extra six inch, galvanized cleats for the masts to add to the other four that I had purchased earlier that summer. I did a good housecleaning and got rid of a lot of things that were lying around, so it looked roomier. I still had that second coat of paint to put on the cabin and the silicone joints to finish. I also wanted to varnish the boomkin.

September 6th, 1997

I spent the day alone on the boat. I had a problem to correct for next spring. The toilet pump handle had been accidentally broken by my brother, and I couldn't empty the waste tank. There was too much resistance in the toilet pump. Vegetable oil would likely fix that. As for the waste tank, I might have to remove and inspect everything. I wondered what I might find … oh, never mind. I continued to houseclean the interior, and Francois made me an all-brass handle for the pump and the vegetable oil worked fine.

September 14th, 1997

I went down to Oka Marina to see a friend and his wife. I needed someone to talk to about boats. They had a thirty four foot, converted schooner. She was made of white pine planking. She had once been two-masted like mine, but with the short mast in front and the long one behind. I admired this couple for their friendliness, respect, and teamwork. They were always together. When they went sailing, it was for two to three days at a time, either week-ends or holiday week-ends.

They invited me out for a sail. Once we were on the lake, Heather insisted on calling my wife at work to come and join us at 4 p.m. There she was at the dock, and we were off again. I steered with a wheel helm for the first time, plus I got to sail his ship. There were winds of 10 knots with gusts of up to 13 knots. *Offwego,* which was their sloop, leaned over easily to a twenty-five-degree angle. The water ran right into the cockpit.

This schooner dated back to 1952, and she weighed in at 6½ tons. She had an 8½-foot beam. She was thirty seven feet overall, with a thirty four foot deck. This explained her excessive heeling. The width was twenty-five percent of her length, which was normal for schooners. The problem was the height of the new mast, had been increased. I found it too high for the boat's width. If the mast had been five feet shorter, she would have been more stable. Some boats have tall masts, but they have a deeper keel. The speed of the boat didn't exceed 4½ knots upwind. With her displacement, she moved as well as expected on the water. She was her own master. I really liked certain things about this boat like the interior which was superbly finished in a bright varnish. The layout was also done in good taste. I could let this boat seduce me as well. *Offwego* was a beautiful boat, but I still liked mine more. I missed my boat that day.

Autumn was here, and so the end of the sailing season was nearing. I was sad. That winter would be a long one. *Mandolin Wind* would become a prisoner of snow and ice. I too started to feel like something was dying inside of me. There was still a lot to do before winter set in, and I didn't have much time. The end of the sailing season was often sad.

# 13. Winter Preparations

October 10th, 1997

Finally the big day was here for the winter preparations. It would be a two-day job. I took down the masts with the help of Marc. Everything went well. We had two sawhorses installed fore and aft of the boat, along with a support in the center. We used the fixed crane technique, and then we tied everything down securely. It took three hours, and we were back at our dock. It was a nice day, but there was not much activity.

I then transferred the trailer from my neighbor's yard to the front of my yard to prepare it to be hauled down to the marina. My van did that part of the job, but I couldn't have hauled this trailer long distance. It must have weighed three thousand pounds. Marc and I cleared off the wire grate, which was welded in place, which was there to provide traction for the bulldozers, tractors, and backhoes that drove on and off of it. It was upon this that I eventually had a cradle made to size and welded in place. I checked the six wheel bearings, and they had all been greased. I would have to buy a tire, a grease cap, and a wheel bearing's inner seal. I had removed all the old wiring. I had also bought the license plate and portable trailer lights.

The following week was the big weekend when all the boats came out of the water. Some 70 or so boats would come out on Friday and around 100 on Saturday, all in the thirty foot class or less. On Sunday, all the boats over thirty feet were hoisted out (another 100). There were four mobile cranes to lift us out of the water.

October 18th, 1997

This was the day we were to haul out the boat. I spent the week running after a few things. All was ready. That morning I installed the wheel with the new tire on the trailer. The ground was covered with frost and it was very cold on the feet. I went into the house to put on warmer boots. My brother arrived at 7:45 a.m. We hooked up the trailer to his van, installed the lights, and I followed him down to the marina (sixty five miles away). We got there around ten in the morning. Even for his larger van, the trailer was quite heavy. Two weeks earlier, I had gone down to the Oka Marina to take apart the old wooden cradle. On the following day, I had him pick up the trailer and haul it to my home so that I could finish the repairs on it. That's when we were convinced that he could haul the trailer, but empty. There was lots of running around.

Trouble began at the hauling out. After two annoying hours of trying to start the Atomic 4, she finally fired up. Even after that, she kept on stalling. Something was wrong. I started the long task of emptying the boat. It was a long walk from the van to the boat and back. Then around 2:45 p.m., Mr. MacSween advised me to move the boat to the haul out area where the crane was. Being shorthanded, I asked him to drive my van back to the haul out location because I would need it to move the trailer. I had removed the old, broken jack (the one that usually come with a trailer), under the tongue of the trailer and replaced it with a few cement blocks. I had a hydraulic jack in the back of the van which I would need to raise or lower the trailer again by its tongue.

I was still having firing problems, then after five minutes or so, the motor fired up. I let it warm up. I put the boat in gear and the motor stalled. I started it again and I put it into reverse. There was no one to help me untie the boat or to guide me out. I backed out slowly in case the motor should stall (there are no brakes on a boat) and she did just that. Panic struck for real now. There were boats tied up behind me. I got her started again and put her into forward gear. It worked. I was ten feet away from the other boats behind me.

As I advanced to the haul out area, I was told to wait. After turning around a couple of times in a circle, the boat stalled once or twice in the midst of all this. I decided to tie up to the forward dock and wait, seeing that the crane on the dock behind was having its problems. I jumped off the boat and headed towards the van. I had to move and back the trailer into its designated spot. I managed that part okay, and I went back to my boat.

I tried to start the motor – nothing doing. So finally, with a volunteer helper on the aft rope and my brother on the forward rope, we backed up the boat to the following dock behind us. I had left my rudder in a position so that when we started to pull the boat backwards, her aft end would try to head out away from the dock. This is what I wanted. The helper on the aft end rope didn't seem to understand that it kept the boat from rubbing against the lower docks. Finally we got there. Now there was just the haul out left to do.

Placing the straps under the hull wasn't easy. Preparing the Tanzer for hauling out was simple, but this boat had very little margin for error, inches maybe. The straps had to be at the exact spots and, with everything happening underwater, we had to guess a bit. Were the straps placed in the right areas? As the boat was lifted out of the water, my heart was beating like mad. There was a risk of breaking the rudder, the propeller, or the shaft. Fear was replaced by satisfaction as the boat rose into the air. I saw that the straps were placed in their proper locations.

Then it came time to lower the boat onto its cradle. My brother and I were the only two there to guide the crane operator who was maneuvering the boat, whereas there should have been three or four of us. Help was scarce. Everybody was taking care of their own hauling out. As the boat was being lowered onto the cradle, one of the cradle pads at the back flipped up into the vertical position and almost pierced the hull. The hull boards flexed about ½ inch before I saw the trouble. After three or four tries, we got her settled in. This was the first time that the pads on the new cradle had been adjusted to fit the hull. Next year it would be simpler. The one favorable thing on my side was that the temperature had warmed up. It had climbed to seventy two degrees F. with a gorgeous sun and no wind. It felt like eighty degrees.

I prepared the motor for winter storage on land at the marina by running the engine to evacuate the water and filling it with antifreeze. I finished taking out the remaining boat equipment, which I would take home to store till the next spring. I washed and scrubbed the hull. I jacked up the three major corners of the trailer and set it on blocks. Then I covered the boat with a tarp, and taped and roped it down. By six p.m., I was finished working, and I was dead tired, more than that, I was beat, exhausted, kaput! There was no one left at the marina; they had already left for the day. I had trouble hanging onto the steering wheel; my arms were so heavy driving home. It was about six thirty p.m. It had been a very hard and stressful day, but it had ended well. The boat was now put away for the winter, or should I say "winterized."

November 12th, 1997

I phoned Mr. Harron to let him know how my season had turned out and to solve a few mysteries.

1st; question in two parts: Did the motor run hot, and how much oil did it take?

The answer was no to the first part, and two quarts because the engine angle of 18degrees was 3degrees over the limit. The engine was positioned at too great an angle. Could this have been the problem?

2nd; question: What is the keel made of?

Answer: mahogany.

3rd; question: Name and address of the former owner?

Answer: Mr. Neil Pride, Smithville, Ontario.

4th; question: Who had designed the boat?

The design was a copy of a Thomas C. Gilmer clipper ship. This designer lived in Maine, USA.

5th; question: Had there ever been any spreaders on the mainmast?

No, but he had been on the verge of making a set. Never saw the day. As I found out later, theoretically there wasn't a need for spreaders, because of a shorter mast and because it was stepped through the deck onto the keel and with the help of extra shrouds.

6th; question: What type of motor was in the boat before?

It had a small, one-piston engine, and it still had the original propeller. This engine turned the propeller shaft slowly.

7th; question: How long did you own it?

Mr. Pride had purchased it in 1972 and had sold it to Mr. Harron in 1991. So, Mr. Harron had owned it for six years before I purchased it from him.

The last bit of information was this: The boat was a cutter rigged ketch with a smaller oak rudder originally. Apparently it was hard to come about in a headwind because of its small rudder. A bigger rudder had been installed for better boat handling. The original jib was on a tiny roller furler that had been installed by Mr. Pride. Mr. Harron bought and installed the bigger Harkin MkII roller furler to replace the other roller furler.

# 14. The Beginning/The *Wanderlust*

November 15th, 1997

I phoned Neil Pride, and we had a long chat. He seemed to be around my age. Neil had named the boat *Wanderlust,* and she was not completely built when he purchased her in 1972 for $300 from a fellow by the name of Henry. Henry had a small business called Henry Boat Works in the boat building industry in the Niagara peninsula area; more specifically, in Port Dalhousie.

In 1968, Henry started building *Mandolin Wind* from wood left over from former projects. He was planning on going down south with her. She was to be a ketch model with a butterfly bow. The boat design was similar to a boat called *Privateer.* The boat was customized for one man. She had a bowsprit of four feet and a boom kin of three feet. She was constructed of double planked cedar on oak ribs. The keel was made of mahogany, and the ribs were made of oak and steam bent. Her length on deck was 30½ feet, and she was 37 ½ feet overall. Her beam was nine feet, ten inches, and her displacement was around nine thousand pounds. She had a lead keel of two thousand pounds and another twelve hundred pounds of steel ballast inside the boat. The mainmast stood thirty five feet above water, and the mizzenmast was thirty two feet above water. The keel had been laid, and all of the ribs on one side and three quarters of the ribs on the other side had already been installed when Henry passed away from a heart attack.

All of his business equipment was sold, naturally; but it took a number of years to settle the ownership of the building where the work on the boats took place. This permitted the new owner of the boat, Mr. Neil Pride, who had bought the boat in 1972, to finish building the boat. Having had some experience in boat building, as he had helped Henry build a 28-foot double chined sailboat he had ordered for himself, Neil had the confidence to take on the job of finishing *Wanderlust* and renaming her Mandolin Wind. He had the blueprints to complete the hull, but not the cabin. Years later, Henry's wife found the rest of the blueprints stuffed in the rafters. The boat was completed in 1976.

The deck and cabin were finished in fiberglass (canvas and epoxy) covered plywood and painted white, and the masts and booms also were painted white. The topside of the hull was orange with a black hull below the water line. The boat looked something like a clipper. Originally, it had a one cylinder, seven h.p. gasoline engine that was built especially for fishing boats.

Around 1991 the boat was purchased by a man named David Harron. He made some changes to her sail plan, had a roller furler installed, and changed the hull color to forest green. He had the rudder increased in size for better control and had the motor changed from a one piston to a four piston Atomic 30 h.p. motor. He demolished the kitchen section to make room for the motor, being that it was much bigger. Mr. Harron then dropped this boat project to pursue another project, a larger boat. He donated the boat to S.A.L.T.S. in exchange for a tax write-off. She was just too much work in his eyes. S.A.L.T.S. put the boat up for sale in the *Boats for Sail* magazine, and the rest is history.

By the time I got this boat in 1997, it was indeed in great need of T.L.C. One piece of vital information: there had been a staysail positioned between the mainmast beginning at the goose neck of the boom and going up to the top front of the mizzenmast. This explained why I had two spare turnbuckles. That night I wrote a letter to Neil recapping everything that we had discussed on the phone. He promised to send me the blueprints, if he could find them, and a booklet by Thomas C. Gilmer on the clipper ship. He mentioned that he had a photo or two of the sail plan of the boat, which he would send me. He also invited me to come and visit his shop.

# 15. A Sense of Being Lost

At the end of 1997, I composed a poem about *Mandolin Wind* and my feelings.

## *Mandolin Wind*

I am lonely; my heart's sad and forlorn,
My life has no meaning, without your strong embrace.
You've gone away, and I begin to mourn,
For loss of charms, in me that have their place.

You're like a vessel from the past, a ghost,
With bounty flowing, that I haven't touched and kissed.
You lured my heart, and now you are my host,
We are of one, and you are sorely missed.

Spring seems so far away, winter's here for good,
And all I have are images, I've kept from yesterday.
You wore your best attire; you set a splendid mood,
I here must waste my fire, until a day in May.

How I desire to be upon you, to satisfy my passion,
To see your towering masts, hold white cloths in place.
Winds whispering in your sails, to send us on a mission,
Through sun and wind and water, elements we must face.

I now know deep within, why of you I am,
You've given me in ecstasy, unselfish love of sailing.
Through power by wind and waves, respect for nature's frame,
I wait for you in these cold times, till once again be sailing.

Guy G. Lemieux
30 December 1997

February 7th, 1998

I went to the boat show with my son, Marc. The temperature was 33 degrees F. I had never seen it this warm in all the years that I had gone to the show. It was always around -10 to -20 degrees F. The show was not impressive. I did notice that there were three Hunter sailboats. This had been a mega show at one time, but not anymore. The problem was that everyone was there to sell their wares. They were not there to generate interest in sailing or sailboats, and my need was for information on the construction of boats. Since I wasn't in the market to buy a boat, I was probably expecting too much.

As for all of the exhibits, I rather enjoyed them. They were certainly interesting and helpful. I did get two helpful tips talking to workers of a marine supply exhibit. One was to have my rusting galvanized cables regalvanized, and the other was to have my mainsail shortened six inches, which would bring an improvement to the sail adjustment and sailboat performance.

I started to plan for the following spring. I would repair the crack in the rear of the keel just above the propeller. It was already reinforced on each side, but I had a feeling that it should be repaired better. Later, I would tune up the motor. I had covered the hull below the waterline with fisherman's red bottom paint. I'd have some touch-ups to do on the green hull and the boot stripe. From there, I would attack the toe-rail and the lifeline supports or railing. I would remove the old toe-rail and install a new one with proper openings for drainage. It would have a mahogany or teak cap for a finish. The balance would be made of laminated cedar. Then I'd varnish the rear of the cockpit and repair the hatches and install the roof rails. I would leave the interior for another time. I also had the steering system to set up. It seemed like a never ending list to attack. Nevertheless, I was looking forward to doing all these repairs; so come on, springtime!

Way back in 1989, I had already begun to think about sailing in exotic places like the Galapagos Islands and the islands of the Caribbean. I had spent all those years reading and planning and dreaming, and I still do. Nonetheless, I began to realize that I was not prepared to set sail and leave my country. There were too many bugs. I didn't know where to start. My first problem was how to prepare myself.

I decided I would start by getting proper training in navigation and accumulating some experience on the sea. I would have to depend on friends, and my own sailing experiences. I would charter a boat with a captain for a couple of weeks so I could practice my seamanship with his supervision for those fourteen days sailing along the St. Lawrence River to the Madeleine Islands. I would take navigation courses that fall with the Canadian Power Squadron, which proved to be interesting and exciting.

I hadn't figured out whether I should use my wooden boat as my future home or get rid of it and buy a steel or fiberglass boat. I didn't know which one would be the least costly and the easiest to maintain. One thing was certain, I would have a boat. But would it be the right one? Should I get rid of the motor in the *Mandolin Wind* and install a diesel motor? What about the wooden masts? Oh, if only there was a club for wooden sailboat owners to turn to.

My next preoccupation was figuring out how I would support myself. Could I make some kind of living? Could I rely on my drafting skills? Could I help people in poor countries to develop their building skills? To do this, I would need to be near waterfront towns, villages, or cities. How about writing articles on the precarious, everyday freestyle life? For this, I would need a computer. Maybe I could get a job with a local newspaper writing or maybe chartering out my boat and my services to people. I could offer my services as a handyman.

My biggest handicap was the fear of leaving my family and friends – leaving for a new and different life. Leaving with only what I knew and understood. At home, everything was so complete, safe, and categorized. How would I cope with loneliness and fear? Why did I want to do this? Why did I want to leave? What was out there for me? What did I expect to gain? I had no idea except that I had this terrible sense of losing out, of shortchanging myself. I wanted my freedom. I wanted to be unleashed from the humdrum of everyday living and venture out to new horizons.

Our time is completely consumed by the necessity of working and producing. We are not given enough time to ourselves to think. This is the biggest bug. No time to think. It could take days of pondering before realizing just the mere idea of a probable project. Life won't give you that time. That's why I had to take walks and talk (think out loud) to myself.

There was no one there who understood me, who could help me thrash out my thoughts. Throughout our lives, we live for our country. We are a commodity, a producer of revenue. You can't leave! You'll get no support – not even moral support! You'll be alone. This is what I had to realize and accept, becoming a man without a country.

My wife did not agree with my thoughts and feelings. I was lost. She didn't want to be a follower. She chose differently. I really needed someone to motivate me, someone who understood me. I had a hard time encouraging myself to follow my dream. I had no one to communicate with on the subject, and when I did, I felt ridiculous again and again, like a dreamer out of touch with reality. Had I not criticized my father of this at the beginning? He'd also had no one to talk to. It seemed that most men who were in quest of a dream were loners. I always had this guilty feeling that I was going to abandon my family. I felt that I was wrong and that I had no right to do this. I actually felt like I was a bad person with no sense of responsibility.

I was afraid to put the wheels in motion. I hesitated. Why did I torture myself? To my thinking, I had very little left to contribute to my daughter's or my two sons' lives. They were all doing well and nearing the end of their education. They would fare well for themselves. I had about two more years to coach them along. I knew what I had to do; it was just a question of doing it. It was a do or die type of thing.

# 16. Renovation, Part Two

I went to Campi Marina to see the boat over the Easter weekend just to have a look. There was hardly anything left of my first winter tarp; it had been torn to shreds by the winter winds. *Mandolin Wind* looked so depressing, so abandoned.

On the 9th of May, the boats were all put into the water with the exception of *Mandolin Wind*. I had her hauled to a lot across the street from my house in St. Colomban. Once the boat was on home turf, I spent my two weeks of vacation time and all of my available weekends working on her. I removed the entire epoxy covered canvass on the foredeck and afterdeck. I cut out three rotten sections of deck plywood. I also removed two side planks from the hull. Naturally, what that meant was I had to remove both layers, as my boat was double planked. I used clear B.C. cedar for the hull and B.C. fir plywood on the deck. I removed the toe-rail and the lifelines and stanchions. I also removed the rub-rail. I sanded the wooden hull approximately one foot down from the deck to inspect it. It seemed fine. I also removed the rear boomkin and all the hatches to have them rebuilt or repaired and painted.

I bought seven boat stands for $300 which I found in the *Boats for Sail* magazine. They were half the price of new ones and in mint condition. I sold my trailer for $250 plus a three-bladed, 12-inch propeller (like a Gori propeller) with a reverse pitch thrown in the deal. When I put it in reverse, the propeller blades reversed direction; and when it was in neutral, the blades flattened out, resulting in less resistance.

September 18th, 1998

The work on the boat was progressing at a snail's pace. In just over two weeks, we had logged approximately 30 hours on fiberglass preparation, plus I had put in 12 hours on repairs on the deck forepeak and a new floor 25" by 25" with a 1" to 0" pitch from the front of the main hatch to the back of the smaller hatch just ahead of it. This was to eliminate the ½ inch of water accumulation.

Next in line was strengthening the crossbeam on the main hatch entrance and having it built up to seal out any water lying on the upper deck. My goal was to make the boat completely waterproof on the deck and cabin top, including the hatches, so far so good. We covered the deck and cabin by double tarping it in the following weeks. That was the end of working on the boat for that season. The rest of the work would have to wait until the following year.

The bowsprit, boomkin, and all the other parts were in the shed. They'd give me something to work on during that winter. This permitted me time to correct little details on the masts and make two spreaders (crosstrees) to replace two others. I could hardly wait.

I estimated that it might take another year to finish the inside of the boat. I was always busy. I had to strengthen the pivoting point of my rudder, which ran through the center of the keel. I had a rub-rail and a toe-rail to build and install. Then I had to sand the whole hull again, caulk some areas, and paint it, adding a boot stripe. Then, last of all, anti-fouling paint. I also had to reinstall all – and I mean all – the hardware topside. I hadn't even touched the inside, which was what bugged my wife the most. The inside was not in pristine condition. Lots of work lay ahead, but I was eager and happy.

December 31st, 1998

The previous year had not turned out as I had thought it would. Every time I looked at the boat, my planned repairs seemed to grow in size and scope. To rebuild, you must start by removing the unwanted. You must get to the keel of a boat before rebuilding it, making sure to do the proper repairs. This was my demon. Let me explain. Of the work I wanted to accomplish on the boat, I would say that about 10% had been done. This took a heavy toll on my self-confidence. The complexity of refitting a boat and the time consumed in doing it was overwhelming. I was only a hobbyist.

I had made mistakable assumptions. For example, I had expected a lot of help from my two sons; but, I guess dreaming was permitted, and I paid the price. My boys had their own lives, and I had neglected that fact. It was my own fault. I did get some help from them, or things would have been slowed down even more. I really needed a roof over the boat so that I could work on it during all kinds of weather; rainy days, hot and sunny days, cold spring days, and autumn days. I finally built an awning forty feet long x thirty feet wide, which kept the sun off of me as well as the falling leaves and pine needles.

What I accomplished over the winter months was acquiring a better understanding of what was in store for me in the way of repairs for the coming season. I became better prepared mentally, and this would give me a fresh start to continue refitting the boat. I did know that she would not be in the water that coming season. I just had too many details to cover. I replaced the shear planking on the topside of the boat and the plywood that needed replacing along with a few reinforcements. I had the cabin roof and deck finished in new fiberglass by an expert. I was now on the right track, building instead of tearing apart.

In the meantime, I would have to finish the toe-rails and the three cabin hatches. The toe-rails were shaped to the boat's curves (in jigs which held the rail parts together) while the glue dried. The last toe-rail section went across the aft end, and this was a tight curve. The first time I took the assembled toe-rail out of the jig, within minutes it sprang apart due to too much tension. Success was achieved on the second try. There was also the main hatch, grab rails, trunk moldings, two side planks, and the binnacle to do. Just that was a lot of work. That would bring the work to about 60% done. I didn't speculate any further on how much work I would get done because of past experiences. I had to have faith in my project, so onward I went. Mind you, at this stage the work was a challenge and becoming interesting.

I was anxious to continue my project, but there would be a slight change in my attitude towards the project. Since my sailboat was out of commission, I intended to sail by other means, such as in a borrowed boat, as a deckhand, or even possibly in a rented boat. I intended to get out once in a while and still enjoy my project.

For now my boat was very well covered for the winter with two polyethylene sheets and two winter tarps. She was on her new stilts just across the street from me. Her masts were laid out onto four sawhorses. This would keep them three feet off the humid ground and level. In the meantime, the boat show was coming up in two months in Montréal, and I needed the winter months to replenish the treasure chest and to think.

January 30, 1999

I discovered that my motor had a reduction gear on it, which allowed the shaft to turn at around 1,500 rpm's. This allowed the boat to have a bigger propeller, such as a 16" x 12". If I removed the reduction gear and changed my prop to a 12" x 9", this would double the rpm's and put less torque on the shaft and therefore less power in the waves.

I cleared out the shed and set up house to work on the boat parts. I started by removing the hardware on the two booms. Then I cleaned off all the paint that had got on the hardware. It looked better afterwards. Then I sanded the round boom clean. Being white, it always looked dirty. I was planning to stain and varnish it. The same went for the second boom, which was rectangular in shape. I intended for it to be round, so out came the planer and belt sander.

I drove down to the Boathouse store to buy a liter of Cétol and a liter of Epiglass, along with some hardener, thinner, and varnish. I also intended to sand and refinish the bowsprit and the boomkin. This would get me closer to spring.

February 2nd, 1999

I left for the Toronto Boat Show at 6:45 p.m. on Friday, the 24th of January. I stayed two evenings at my sister's. Road conditions were dangerous when I left Québec because of a snowstorm, which later changed to sleet and then rain. I was lucky, as I had the wind at my back. By the time I reached Kingston, it was smooth driving. I crossed quite a few wipeouts on the highway as well as an overturned pickup truck. This was always a bad stretch, driving along Highway 401. I started driving at forty five mph. for some time and eventually I reached sixty five mph. I clocked in at 1:30 a.m.

The two days I spent with my sister were pleasant. We caught up on all the current and social events that Friday and Saturday night, and I made her my special breakfast, a micro-egg, to start the day off on Saturday morning. She then drove me down to the CNE (Canadian National Exhibition) grounds, which was where the show was. I walked around the boat show from 10:00 a.m. until 5:15 p.m. I must have gone around the entire show at least three times.

There were at least 20 big sailboats, thirty feet and up, and 30 or so tiny sailboats as well. There was the twenty six foot McGregor, which I was anxious to see. It pleased me very much to see it, as it had a number of very convenient features. It was trailer-able, which was a great commodity, when the time comes to maintenance and minimizing marina costs. It sleeps 5-6, has a nine inch draft, can motor up to twenty two mph. out of a storm, and has no through hulls.

I talked to the people from a boat building school called "The Pier," where they give weekend classes on how to build little wooden boats. This excited me, and I was even toying with the idea of taking their course to improve my understanding and craftsmanship to make me a better boat worker. I purchased "Fugawi," a software program used to read and plot navigational charts, which can then be downloaded to a GPS or can be used to navigate directly from a computer. Now all I needed were some charts. I saw many things that interested me, and came out of this show feeling a little brighter. I enjoyed the show and also appreciated time spent alone with my sailor's thoughts. At 5:15 p.m. I took the 20-minute walk back to my sister's, still caught up in my thoughts. After all that walking, I rested for the remainder of the evening.

Sunday, after good-byes, I left at 9:30 a.m. and went down to Queen's Quay to see the boats that were docked there over the winter. There were about a dozen of them. There were the square riggers, *True North, Pathfinder,* and *Fair Play,* amongst the other types of boats. They all seemed so forlorn, lost, and unwelcoming. I'm sure that inside these boats there was a warm stove burning, an oil lantern lit, and hot coffee – all giving off pleasant odors – along with a good cigarette. I had quit smoking, but I still enjoyed the smell of a cigarette burning. After fifteen minutes of gazing, accompanied by silent thoughts, I sauntered back to my car and left for home in a saddened mood because of the weekend coming to a close. I took the Ivy League drive and stopped at a marina along the way to look at the boats. I also stopped to look at a schooner, which was winterized, along with her winter tenants. She looked inviting. I then continued on my way, gazing at the St. Lawrence River as I daydreamed about the renovations I would make to my boat, such as fiberglassing the keel so that she would sail faster. I got home at around 4:00 p.m.

Spring, 1999

I talked to my engineering friend and asked him if I could rent his sailboat for two weeks during the coming summer. He said yes, and all I needed to know now was how much. It was more than a fair price, $150 per week. I had already started saving money for the occasion.

Finally summer came and Jacinthe and I invited another couple to come spend a week's holiday on this sailboat which I had rented for the occasion. It was a twenty six foot Contessa with a long keel that was a joy to sail. They were old friends of mine from my teenage years. We crossed the Lake St. Francis and stayed in Cornwall for a couple of days.

Near the end of our vacation, we were on our way back from Cornwall when I gave the tiller to Mike, my best buddy. He was tickled pink. Charlene and Jacinthe wanted to sunbathe, so they lay down on the front deck near the bow balcony. From behind us came two big motor cruisers on the swift. They passed us on each side and, seeing that they were going in the same direction. I told Mike not to worry, that we were only going to get some waves, nothing dramatic!

Well, the two waves hit us simultaneously, square in front, one on each side, and the water gushed over the bow onto the boat. You never saw two sunbathers get up so fast in your life! I was laughing out loud, and even Mike joined me; but Charlene was fuming. She ran to the back of the boat where we were and started scolding her husband. I told her that it was my fault, and then I took a verbal beating. Laughing time was over. No matter how hard I tried to explain to Charlene that it was a fluke and the chance of that ever happening again was a bit rare, nothing could calm her down. I was lucky that Jacinthe had taken it all in stride and finally was able to calm Charlene down. *Phew!* I thought I was dead. That holiday almost ended on a sour note.

As for my boat, I hoped to finish the exterior that summer and the interior during the winter. She had to be ready to go into the water by the year 2000, come hell or high water! I didn't intend on replacing any mechanical parts on the boat. Although they were not top of the line, they did the job. My intention was to sail the boat and make replacements whenever necessary. Then if I had any spare money, I'd think about esthetic replacements.

# 17. The *Osprey*

December 17th, 2000

In 1999 and 2000, I worked very hard trying to finish the renovation of my boat. I hired a boy of 15 or 16 years of age, Jean-Paul, to do all the tedious chores, such as painting and cleaning the boat. The exterior went well, but the inside was much harder. Because of low headroom in the v-berth, most of the painting of the ceiling, the forward compartment, and even the sides had to be done lying on one's back; and then lying on one's stomach to paint the bunks. The back section was easier except for the ceiling, which was especially hard if you were taller than five feet. Jean-Paul, my busy bee, who wasn't so little, had a change of heart and went to work elsewhere. One week later, he and his father came to see me. Jean-Paul wanted to come back to work for me. He liked my friendship better than that of his new boss. It certainly wasn't the pay. We worked together all summer, and we got along just fine. My daughter had given him piano lessons for about eight years. Today this young lad has a master's degree in trumpet playing. I got to like Jean-Paul very much because he was a very well-mannered and an easy going boy.

I worked on *Mandolin Wind* every day I could, taking only three days off the entire year, aside from my two-week-long sailing holiday, to do something other than work on the boat. On the 6th of December, 2000, I was discouraged by some nagging news. The property owners gave me a notice to move my boat by May 15. They were planning on installing a swimming pool.

May 4th, 2001

That spring I was short on ideas, such as where was I going to store my boat. I had another neighbor, who was more than willing to lend me a piece of his land just in front of my home at no charge; then bang! I was refused access to this property because of some political issues. That hurt. Back to the drawing board I went.

I missed my May 15th deadline to move the boat. The landowners were quite annoyed and threatened to burn the boat if I didn't move it. I called the Oka Marina owner, Claude, and asked him if he would move my boat to his yard temporarily until I could find another location. On June 3rd; the boat was hauled back to Oka. I tried to work on my boat but with very little success. I couldn't install a tent; so, when it rained, I couldn't work. I built a makeshift awning over the cockpit, but because of the sun, it was just too hot under there. I took it down three weeks later.

During my stay at Oka, I met this chap, who was around 71 years old and was living on his boat, a Cal 25 yacht which was up on a cradle right next to my boat. He called his boat the *Osprey*. His name was Leonard Waters, and he spoke just like a guy out of a western movie. He even had the same cowboy gait. He wore a black Pittsburgh Pirate baseball cap.

Osprey in fine shape for a forty year old sailboat

Getting ready for the start

Roxanne and the girls leaving the dock for the big race

Osprey head to head with Hippocamp. Roxanne at the helm and
Francois working the sails.

He went grocery shopping every two days because of storage problems. For this errand, he used an old, yellow ten-speed and a knapsack to carry his groceries. During the day he would lie on his aluminum chair lounged under a makeshift awning in the cockpit. He had a tiny radio when listening to baseball games. I kidded him a lot, and I even sketched a picture of him.

He was there primarily to sell his boat. He had decided to sell his boat because of a very bad hip that hindered his movements. He had almost fallen into the water because of it. He was waiting to have an artificial hip joint installed. He had a For Sale sign on the front of it that read "$5,000 she's yours". He was relying strictly on passers-by, whom were quite rare.

During the last ten years, he had sailed, lived, and slept on the lake, only coming into a marina to get his groceries at a general store. During the winter months, he had stayed in an old trailer camper in Mont St. Sauveur, where he would cross-country ski. He was quite the sailor. Some of his stories would curl your hair, and he was hard to beat on a tack.

Father's day came around, and my three young adult friends (kids) and my wife came to take me out for supper. I was working on my boat when they arrived. I introduced them all to Len. After a few moments, Len came over to me and asked, "Why don't you buy the kids my boat?" I told him that I hadn't thought of that. We were leaving to go to the restaurant when Len called me over and said that he'd take $3,000 if we were interested.

We went for supper at a place just next door, and I made a proposition to my three kids. If they were interested, we could make a four-way partnership, $750 each, with my share given to them as an incentive. So a deal was closed, and everyone was happy. My kids now had their own personal boat; boating would be their hobby and sport. I was happy because the kids would be around more often. Len was happy as well. He could now move back to his trailer.

I spent the rest of the summer working on their boat and sailing it with them. It was just too darn hot to work out in the direct sunlight on *Mandolin Wind*. On one occasion I nearly fainted, and that was enough. By Labor Day weekend, I had decided to sell *Mandolin Wind* and buy another boat, one that I could sail immediately. I was getting tired of all the problems and renovations. I was tempted by my children's toy. I almost offered to buy it, but then I changed my mind. I started looking for a shed or a barn or a garage where I could shelter my boat and work on it at the same time.

Buying the *Osprey* turned out to be one of the best things that I had done; it motivated, or coerced, my children into boating. From that day on, they became more involved in the family sport as well as sharing their hobby with their friends. There was never a dull moment for them.

This is what I wanted to pass on to them. This was a way of exchanging good fellowship and harmony while working as a team. They were entwined in a closer relationship amongst themselves, and their father also benefited from the rich moments that he shared with them. You couldn't buy the love and friendship that we shared, and this acquisition was just an access key. The summer passed by quickly. Sometimes letting go of one's own boat a little can do marvelous things. I acquired a renewed interest and a desire to continue the renovation of *Mandolin Wind*.

# 18. A New Workshop

Fall 2000

The next five years would be amongst the happiest years of my life. Finally I found a place for my boat; it was only 10 minutes from my home. My former boss had an uncle who had an all metal barn for his farm equipment. It was in the shape of a domed half circle and was made of corrugated, galvanized steel. It was forty feet long, which was just long enough. There was barely six inches left to spare between my boat and the wall. It was thirty feet wide and twenty four feet high. He was willing to rent it to me for $200 per month, a good price. By the end of September, I was moved in. It wasn't heated, but it was well ventilated, with vents at each end. Whenever it rained or snowed, my boat was kept dry while I worked on her. For a second time, I finished sanding and scraping off the old paint from the two masts. They were now ready to be stained and varnished. The work on the booms was done, and they were beautiful. I would now put on new galvanized rigging and whatever was needed.

My two sons and I carried the masts onto a school bus and had them transported from my home to their new home, which we called "the boathouse." The weight of the masts was too much for me, and I compressed a disc in my back moving them and I was in pain for a couple of months. The year before, there had been five of us to move the masts; but this year we were only three. We carried the masts through the back door of the bus and on to the farthest point forward, where we laid them on the floor. They still stuck out the back some six feet or so. The longer mast measured thirty five feet.

My spirit to continue renovating and refitting *Mandolin Wind* had been rekindled. I would do as much as I could that winter to make up for time lost from the past summer. My other obligations made it hard at times, especially when my wife insisted; but I understood her. The previous summer, I had installed two mahogany doors that were thirty inches in height, which I had made at the shop where I worked. They were for the forward v-berth. I also installed twin shelves, five feet long, and redid the floor in that area. The v-berth was starting to look shipshape. Then I installed the ship's wheel and doghouse. While I was still at the marina, I'd had two sail covers, three hatch covers, and two lee cloths made of a material called *Sumbrella,* in forest green. I had a steering wheel and the doghouse cover made as well.

I continued to work on my ship, and I thanked God for reigniting my interest in her. I knew that someday she would sail again. I had just started my fourth course, my junior navigator's course, which was very interesting but would take two years to complete. I'd never imagined how much fun it would be to sight and read the stars, sun, and moon. It had become a new hobby for me. I started to scan the sky with my binoculars. I even spotted three of Jupiter's moons! I bought the software called Starry Night and this gave me an added motivation for my navigation course. I found the galaxy called Andromeda completely by chance. The Pleiades were so beautiful to see. I used 10-50 power binoculars, which I liked better than a telescope. The stars and planets are easier to keep in view with binoculars because they move at a rate of 15 degrees per hour. I had discovered two completely new interests, navigation and the stars. I was anxious to sail *Mandolin Wind* again and to enjoy her companionship. I could see her every day now that she was a bit closer to home.

## 2001/2002

I must start by saying that during the winter months, it was so cold in the boatshed. It was unbearable. There was no way to heat this place because it was so huge, made of all metal, and had no insulation. There were big air vents at each end. There were also birds in the place. I managed to concentrate and work on the masts. I applied six coats of varnish by having a kerosene heater placed under the part of the mast that I was staining or varnishing. I would stain or varnish three foot segments, at a time, doing only the top side, until I reached the end. Then, two days later, I would roll the mast over half a turn to do the other side. I got it done by the 4th.

of January. Then I closed up shop for the winter. Some days it dropped to minus 18 degrees Fahrenheit, and some nights it dropped to minus 31.

## 2002

I opened up the boathouse around mid March. I was anxious to get started. I spent a day or two making assessments and prioritizing the things that I had to accomplish. The list was still long, but it was getting shorter. I was really lucky because, with all my tools in place, it was much easier to get to work. I didn't have to put them away at the end of the day or even at the end of the year. I had my stock on hand and a setup of good lighting and work benches. I felt at home, better than I could have possibly wished; although, there were many times when I was lonely. To counter that, I would listen to the radio as I worked. Here, I was in my own bubble, lost in my inner thoughts, answering to no one.

## 2002/2003/2004

In the boathouse, I worked approximately 80 working days per year for those three years. There were so many things to do that I stopped listing them. I've mentioned just a few in the following pages. I hired a master electrician to make a custom electrical panel with all the hookups from the batteries, battery selector, power converter, and power sources for the G.P.S., cell phone and handheld V.H.F. radio, a.m./f.m. radio, and boat lighting. He worked three or four days for me and it cost me a pretty sum but it was well worth it.

He also checked out my Atomic 4 motor and got it running. I had another worker come in to sand the bottom of the hull and apply two coats of antifouling. I had parts made out of stainless steel to make the rudder sturdier, because the former owner had increased its size for better handling but not its support. I started by making a wooden working model, or pattern, and then I brought it down to the machine shop to have it duplicated. It was a very efficient design.

There were brass fixtures all over the boat. I traded my winches for Francois', because his were of brass. Francois was studying for his bachelor's degree in industrial engineering, which he later finished. His talent served me well on my boat. He buffed up the winches that were all tarnished from years past (and this took a lathe) and then lacquered them as well. He made three decorative plates with *Mandolin Wind* machined into them. There was one for each side of the cabin top and a smaller one for the back of the doghouse. I painted the engraved lettering forest green, the same color as the hull.

There were brass plates on every step of the companionway, to protect the brightly varnished mahogany steps, and even on the mahogany caps of the two toe-rails, for protection when boarding and leaving the ship. I bought my son new stainless steel rails, or tracks, for adjusting his sheet blocks, which controlled the genoa. In return, I received his brass ones. Then there were the port and starboard lights. Mine were plastic and his were brass. We also exchanged these. The list was long. I bought a windlass to raise and lower the anchor manually that was made of solid brass, and this was my masterpiece!

The interior of the boat looked like that of a new ship. The countertop in the galley was Formica with a special paintbrush effect in different shades of green bordered by a thick mahogany belt across the front edge, which was also brightly varnished. The old stainless steel sink looked like new, along with the taps. My wife made new celery colored bunk cushions; and two years later, I had cream colored, textured curtains installed that gave an added twist. There was a golden, ¼-inch rope tied in a reef knot in the center of each curtain. The floorboards were of thick, brightly varnished mahogany planking; and the sidewalls (the hull areas) were finished with white, painted boards alternated with brightly varnished mahogany boards, all three inches wide; an added luxury. There were two new mahogany hatches, one for the lazaret and one for the sail storage area in the front. There was also a special hatch in the shape of a house roof. It had bulletproof, Plexiglas windows and protective, brass rails. There was also a new companionway with two new doors and a new coach roof all out of mahogany. The list ran on and on. This boat was my pride and joy.

I spent three years in the boatshed, 240 days of work, including summer holidays, weekends, and all of the annual holidays, not counting the other four years that I had worked on the boat. I never worked during the week, because I would have stopped enjoying what I was doing. I had to keep my work on *Mandolin Wind* a hobby. Sometimes during the weekend I would arrive at the boatshed with a Tim Horton coffee in hand and spend the next hour contemplating and admiring the beauty of this boat. I had done right by not selling it. I was alone all the time except on rare occasions when I really needed help. I rather liked it this way, listening to my classical music on the radio.

I never spent my family's budget on the boat; all the money came from winter jobs such as drawing plans for an outside company, working extra hours on 3d drawings for my boss's catalogue. The only drawback was that I was home only in the evenings seven days a week. This worked out fine because my wife worked evenings only during the weekend.

2004

The New Year had arrived. I booked a place at the Oka Marina, and my boat's christening date was advanced by a sudden separation, later followed by a divorce from my wife. I had it coming, and what an unhappy event. I wasn't one for hurting people, but I certainly had here. I put my shoulder to the grindstone and accelerated my work output.

# 19. Return to Her Natural Element

My first priority was to get the boat into the water. Claude, the marina owner, and his son came and picked up *Mandolin Wind* with their truck that had a forty foot platform bed. It was all hydraulically powered. I was rushing against time to tie up all the loose ends necessary to prepare for the forty mile ride back to the marina. Even my newly separated wife showed up. She was still happy for me, and without acknowledging it, probably still felt sad about how our situation had turned out; and so did I. She wished me luck.

Claude fired up the diesel on the truck and gently pulled the boat out of the boatshed, which would become just a barn again. I had to remove the bow pulpit on top of the bowsprit so that the boat could pass under the barn door. Then I had to fix it back in its place for the road trip. There was the matter of seven boat stands to carry in the back of the pick-up truck as well, and two masts to tie onto the side of the trailer. After the boat was all loaded up, Jacinthe left for work. As the truck was leaving the farm, it hung a sharp left turn around a big apple tree, and the tree broke off one of the boat's stanchion posts. That was the only mishap on the way to Oka.

A few of my friends were there to greet me when we got to Oka. They were surprised to see the boat in such a beautiful state. She was gorgeous! The boat was placed in the yard for a few days so I could do the last checks, which all went well. It was now time to place her in her true element, water. We kept her in the straps for 24 hours to let the planks swell up. A wooden boat is not waterproof until the hull planks have swelled up tight by its being in water. Water was coming into the boat slowly, and it became alarming when it rose to three inches above the floorboards. The pump was running all this time. After two hours, the pump was beginning to win; so we set the boat completely in the water and there she stayed overnight. I stayed with her for a while, kind of babysitting her, and left when I could see that everything was just fine.

The next day I came back and started up the engine and steered the boat to her slip. For two weeks I worked on the rigging of the two masts. I was alongside the marina haul out area with my masts again on four horses. The view was a beautiful change of scenery, looking out at the boats and the lake in the background. All summer long I lived on that boat until mid-October, when she was hauled out of the water for the winter. I had the greatest time sleeping on the boat that I'd had in a long time. I imagined myself in another era. I had breakfasts, lunches, and suppers on board.

I spent the next two weeks cutting and crimping and fitting the galvanized cables. This was the hardest part. Near the end of the day my arms would shake when I would crimp an end. Then I proceeded to install pulleys, rope guides, and antennae. There was no room for errors. Then new halyards and blocs and so forth were installed. I had the masts hoisted aboard the boat and proceeded to install them, and then I installed all the rigging. Once that was done, I had to fine tune it. The next step was to install the sails and check them for final adjustments. I had two sails cut by a professional sail maker to a proper fit.

The motor continued its old habit of stalling. The yard mechanic had no time for me. He only worked on the tourist boats. I finally pleaded with him to come and help me out. Two days and $600 later, he was done. The boat ran a minute then stalled. I was furious.

I went and sat in the boat and started to empty out a drawer of stuff when I ran across two old fuel filters. I took one in my hand and blew on the one end, and, man, what a cloud of dust that came out of it. As I looked at it, I pondered for a moment. Could a blocked fuel filter be the cause of all these problems? I went to a garage and bought the same filter and installed it. I started up the motor, and it ran properly. I realized later that the fuel tank was full of sediment. After a few weeks, the fuel filter became congested again. Every 30 seconds or so that I ran the engine, the problem would re-occur. I installed a new fuel filter and a new temporary fuel tank, and the problem stopped. I never told the mechanic what the problem was.

I then had a sail cover sewn onto the genoa to protect it from U.V. rays. I got to sail the boat on a number of occasions during that last half of the sailing season, as I kept doing little things. I even put a pumpkin on the front of the boat on Halloween for the neighbor's kids on the other boats to see. They sang upon my request and I handed out candies. This was pretty close to living my dream of freedom. I didn't work that year. I spent the remainder of my summer sailing in the warm, gentle winds and breezes. I couldn't get enough of it, sailing morning until night and later sometimes.

It was such a pleasure to *let Mandolin Wind* take me out into the wind and water. She was so graceful and inviting. One look at her and her majestic flair would seduce you in a flash, and you wanted to come aboard. You wanted to share her secrets and her poetry. When she wore her suit of sails, you were drawn to her like a magnet. She'd rock you amongst the waves that sang lullabies so sweet they would almost put you to sleep. I went out sailing a lot with *Mandolin Wind* during those last three years.

I slept and cooked and lived on board for three full sailing seasons. Some nights it would drop to 7 degrees Celsius, and I would set the little electric heater to "On," to keep me warm. Sometimes I didn't want to get up. It was like I was in my own little world. Cooking and eating became a new pleasure. I would make eggs over easy in the electric oven along with some toast and coffee. My little oven cooked just about anything. It was a challenge using it. I would use the exterior, stainless steel barbecue on the rear balcony rail to cook the greasy stuff, or when I was at anchor. I didn't have to make the bed in the morning; I would just roll up the sleeping bag and push it behind the back rest of my couch, along with my pillow. Cooking took a bit longer, as well as washing the dishes. As for showering and shaving, I would go to the service area or jump into the lake.

There were always polite, curious people inquiring about the boat. She attracted a lot of attention. Whenever I had to leave the boat for a day or longer, I never tired of turning around and taking one last, long look at her from above the pier. I'd scrutinize her two masts with the booms wrapped in sails, all bundled up in green sail covers. Then I'd spot the new boom at the front of the boat with its staysail also wrapped and covered. To the front of this, there was the genoa, all rolled like a window blind with the green sail cover rolled neatly around it. Just behind it was the stumpy windlass, all polished in brass, sitting atop the glistening, mahogany bowsprit. Beneath the bowsprit, there was a support projecting horizontally with the bowsprit and downwards along the keel that strengthened and supported it. Though there was none on *Mandolin Wind,* usually there was a maiden in the form of a bust attached to this section, especially on older seafaring ships, forever searching the seas ahead for the safest passage. The transom bore a huge ribbon banner carved out of wood with *Mandolin Wind* carved into it.

I would take a look at the masts, which were stained a dark cherry color and brightly varnished, with the top four feet painted white. This gave me a better idea of their heights when passing under such objects as low bridges or electrical wires. The cockpit was stained and varnished the same color as the masts. I would notice the three varnished hatches and the companionway, all covered in their forest green cloth covers; and the long, forest green cockpit cushions and lee cloths. The stout doghouse, sitting between the doubled boomkin, was also covered in green Sumbrella cloth. As a final touch, the toe-rail cap, also stained and brightly varnished, was a perfect match for the boat. All this wood created a nice contrast to the pure white deck and the brass fixtures on the boat.

The round and oblong portholes were fabricated in brass by Francois. The boarding steps, cabin stairs, and the side name plates, all in brass, the navigation lights were of brass. The clock, barometer, hooks, door knobs, door locks, drawer knobs, and mirror were also made of brass. In fact, every metal part on the boat was brass, even the hinges. There was a wheel helm made of mahogany with a brass center bolted down with a big brass nut some two inches in diameter. Once I was satisfied, and only then, would I turn around and walk away. This boat was my heart and soul. Every time I left her, a part of me stayed behind. Nothing could ever replace this boat, for all my energy and hope and love had been put into this "toy," as Dad would have mentioned, "they're exactly that, just toys".

Near the end of the fall that first year, I was sleeping on board *Mandolin Wind,* all snuggled up in my sleeping bag, when I woke up needing to pee. So I went out onto the deck to relieve myself of my overloaded plumbing. As I walked on the deck near mid-ship, I stood facing the water. It was very dark, and the deck was wet and cold. I didn't want to pee on my boat, so I leaned a bit forward. As I finished what I had started, I lost my footing and began to fall backwards when my foot shot out from underneath me and rammed right into the toe-rail drain. It had a vertical separation that was just thin enough to have slipped between my second and third toe and with such force that it sent me dancing on one foot and wailing. I fell onto the cabin top in throbbing pain. I dreaded looking at my toe. I finally hobbled back into the boat and lay on my bunk and stayed this way until the following morning.

Half dozing, I suddenly bumped my toe against the bunk rail. The pain was excruciating. My toe had started to turn black. I thought of going to the hospital and then decided against it. Broken toes they don't fix. I limped about for a couple of days, and I had a nice black toe. I had to go shoeless for a short while, but everything went back into place. All in all, I suffered for about two years. Beware sailors! Wear nonslip shoes on the deck, and don't pee off the deck 1) in the dark, 2) shoeless, or 3) on rainy nights or if there's a lot of dew on the deck.

Some of the rewards of sailing a beautiful Texas sunset.

# 20. *Sanctuary II & Cornish Crabber*

January 2003

One day I saw a little sailboat for sale on the Internet that had everything going for her. She had sheer lines and a nice transom. She had a dark green hull, a cream colored deck and cabin, and teak trim. The boat, a Kittiwake, was not only a good sailer, as it turned out, but was just one magnificent little ship. She was in Texas, just the kind of place that I was looking for to spend some winter time away from Quebec. I purchased an airline ticket and went down to Houston.

The following morning, I went to Don's Yacht Brokerage, which was on NASA Road 1. There I got the lowdown on the Kittiwake, and, after that, Don and I went out to have a look at her at the Blue Dolphin Marina. She was a sloop with a long keel and a shallow draught. When we were done there, we drove back to the agent's place of business. I didn't make a commitment right away, but instead returned on my own to take a closer look at the boat. I checked her out from stem to stern, taking at least 100 pictures. The boat was well equipped and smart. The motor, a Nissan 5 hp, was new.

Don let me crash on a beautiful 33-foot cruiser (which was up for sale), for the duration of my stay. I spent the night on the bunk writing notes and looking over all the pictures. For wheels, I bought an 18-speed mountain bike on which I traveled everywhere within a five mile radius. I returned to the broker and bought the boat the following day.

That day and the next, I returned to make a list of everything, and I mean every nut and bolt and piece of equipment, plus the condition of everything. I had found my boat for the winter holidays. On the last day of my trip, when I returned to the broker, Don introduced me to a gentleman who was also interested in the *Kittiwake*. This fellow had also come there to buy the boat. He was too late by one day, but we shook hands and talked.

He was an astronaut from the Johnson Space Center, which was three or four miles away. That was the year that a shuttle had exploded upon reentry into the earth's atmosphere. This astronaut was in charge of around 3,500 people who were recovering all the items they could find that had been part of the spaceship. It was a tedious job for them, scouring the countryside to collect bits and pieces. I will never forget all the flowers and flags that were placed at the entrance gate to the Johnson Space Center. It was sad. I passed by every morning on my bicycle heading to Denny's for breakfast.

I got to take *Sanctuary II* (this is the sailboats name), out for a motored ride on the last day of my trip. I didn't have time to sail her. I was too busy setting and verifying the sails, and everything else. Everything checked out, but I could have used a couple of extra days. I made arrangements for the transfer of documents and dockage fees for a year. After I had completed everything, I flew back to Canada with a lot to think about. I had to be clear on my goal first of all. I would have *Mandolin Wind* in Quebec for the summer and *Sanctuary II* in Texas for the winter months. I wanted a winter refuge from the snow, and I believed I had found it.

The following year, I made a list of all the things I had to do. With the help of Jacinthe, it seemed that it was going to work out. In 2004, I drove down again on a two-week holiday to finish the preparations on the boat. I ate and slept on the boat as I worked on her. For two nights, after I had painted the inside of the boat, I slept in the van, which was so full of gear that there was barely any room left for air. I managed to take her out sailing on three occasions, and she was a sheer pleasure in every way. I was connected to her now.

I would light up a lantern at night, hang it outside on the rear balcony rail, and daydream of being there during future holidays. I listened to a radio station that played all the old, nostalgic hits from the 50's and 60's. I was so excited when I first went out on *Sanctuary 11*. I liked the way she handled as I followed the buoys out into the Galveston Bay. It was a huge bay, around twenty five miles in diameter. There were fishing nets in many areas, and oil rigs as well. It was impressive to see such a strange contraption out on the water in the middle of nowhere. There were many shrimpers at work also. These were all new scenes to me. That day I sailed until nightfall. As I was returning through the channel buoys, there was this golden sunset. It was such a beautiful sight. I was in another world. I took the most beautiful sunset picture ever.

The second time I set sail, I just zigzagged in every direction, following my charts and familiarizing myself with the area. I spent the day just feeling my way around with the wind. It was so peaceful. I wished that I could have shared my day with someone. There were lobster pots in many places, so I had to be wary. There was also this huge catamaran. The captain and I waved a hand to one another as we crossed paths. We were quite a ways from the other sailboats. Actually, we were right next to the cargo shipping lane.

On the third and final day, I got to sail from Seabrook to Texas City. I borrowed a handheld G.P.S. and with *Sanctuary 11*, I just carved my way through the water. She really did handle well. I was taking the boat to Leon's Marina near Texas City. I sailed in and out all along the shoreline. Once there, two of my friends helped me to lower the mast and secure everything for the night. The next day, with a pivoting crane, they lifted the boat onto a trailer that I had purchased. I could haul it anywhere I wanted to now. My friend trailered it to a storage area, where I tarped it up for the following year. Then I headed back to Canada, a mere twenty five hundred mile drive.

On my return trip, I was near Memphis when I decided to take a scenic route, since it would be a much shorter distance to travel. It was about 2:30 p.m. when I took this highway. The countryside was very well kept, and the road was smooth. There were no tractor trailers allowed. After nightfall, I saw a deer. As I drove along, I spotted another one and then another. I was so impressed that I started counting them. I counted one hundred and thirty two in all, and I know that I missed some. There was some standing in the ditches and on the side of the road. There were also some on the road, which made me stop. It was incredible! I had to drive around thirty to sixty mph. to be able to see them ahead of time. There were stragglers and groups of as many as 6-7 at a time. You could see their white tails or their glowing eyes. When I came to the end of this highway, it was 1:30 a.m. The trip had taken three hours longer than planned. All along the highway right to Cleveland, I saw deer that had been killed by passing vehicles, lying along the side of the road. Scenes like that you never forget – the beautiful and the not so beautiful.

Kittiwake heading out in Galveston bay

Kittiwake at the dock in Texas.

In 2005 I returned to Texas to my boat. My bright idea about winter holidays was not working out. With my wife and I just newly separated, I had new plans on the drawing board. I had decided to bring *Sanctuary II* back to Canada. I went down to Texas for the third time, this time in my Cherokee jeep. I hauled 2½ tons of boat with my Cherokee with all the ease in the world. I had everything I needed to live down south, even a job, but sometimes responsibilities and commitments make us take a different path; and sometimes life's path isn't so clear. I never thought that, much later on, love would be my Achilles' heel. Today I do have some regrets for not going on my voyages; but then again, maybe I wasn't ready. Complete freedom carried a big price for me to pay, emotionally.

This boat was very handsome, and it was well equipped for sailing and living aboard. It had three teak hatches. The splash boards were made of teak. The sails were brand new with ribs to prevent them from flapping. The deck was cream in color, and the hull was forest green. It had a teak toe-rail and bowsprit. What I liked the most about this little boat was that it had a bench right on the rear balcony as well as a single seat on the bow pulpit. This in turn, was on top of a short two-foot bowsprit. This little boat had lazy jacks and halyard jamming cleats. The list was quite long in regards to amenities. It had a new 5 hp motor, a solar panel, and so forth. I really liked sailing this little boat. It had just the right amount of balance and weight and length.

Sailing can come with all kinds of secondary effects. On my last trip to the states, I was stopped one night for speeding. I was going at least one hundred mph. I was on my way back to my motel room when I was intercepted by the police. I was taken to the municipal jail, where I was booked. When I was first brought to the jail, I was handcuffed and a police officer emptied my pockets. I went to reach behind me, and he grabbed my hand and said, "What do you think you're doing, sailor boy?" I replied that I meant no harm; it was just that I had a marlin knife in my belt pouch. He got the knife out and gestured to it, "This?" I said yes, and that I only wanted to help out. I had never been in jail before. I had a horrible night. I had no blankets, no pillow, and I felt cheap on top of it all. The next day, Saturday, I was arraigned. I was charged with reckless driving, and the judge did not set bail. It would have allowed me to bail myself out at that point. He mentioned that it being a federal law it was not in his jurisdiction.

I was transferred to the Galveston County Jail the following day. What a sickening place. Things turned from bad to worse when a male nurse came to talk to me to prepare a medical and psychiatric report for me. One of his questions was, "You ain't goanna die on me, are you?" I made him repeat the question, because I didn't believe what I had heard. I asked him how long I had to stay in jail before I would have a chance to get out, and he told me that it could be as long as three months. Oh boy, I didn't feel so good.

In theory, it takes someone on the outside of the prison to bail you out. I asked a prison guard how I could get myself out. He told me all I had to do was make a call to a bail bondsman, and the bail bondsman would do the rest. This sounded fine and I asked him which one I should call. He said, "Look on that piece of paper you have there." There were five different ones listed. Again, I asked who would be the best hope? He told me that it would most likely be the closest one. There was one across the street from the jail. I was allowed one call. The bail bondsman took all the necessary information and my Visa card number over the phone. They verified my credit card payment of $1600 plus $250 in fees. Half an hour later, a bail bondsman came to the jail, filled out the papers, and posted my bail. I was free to leave!

While I was being transferred from the municipal jail in a police car, there was this young woman riding along who was a bit rough looking. She was still in booking when I was released. When she saw me leaving, she accosted me in an angry tone, asking how I had gotten them to release me. I saw a side of the law I don't ever want to see again. However, I was relieved that things had worked out all right.

It was 11 pm, and I was forty miles or so from Kemah, where my car had been impounded. I couldn't seem to get any help getting out there. Finally, I came across this African-American fellow who was going that way. He agreed to take me there for 40 bucks, but he had to stop by his house first to let his wife know where he was going. I tell you, being driven by a stranger in the dead of night, not knowing where he is going to take you can be pretty scary. But it ended well. I got to my destination safe and sound. The driver had to wait for me to pay him, as I didn't have a cent on me.

I rang at the impound gate, and luckily they let me in. They agreed to let me fetch my wallet from the Cherokee, and I went and found my wallet where I had hidden it and paid them and the driver. The lady at the towing company was around my age, though she looked much older. She gave me a card with The Lord's Prayer on it. She told me to read the prayer in times of need. Finally I was on my way back to the hotel where I had been staying, and thank God, not the jail. Back at the hotel, the owner had removed my baggage from my room and put it in a storage area. I retrieved my baggage, and paid for one final night's stay before leaving in the morning. I slept until early morning, and then got up and got ready for my trip back home.

My boat was locked in the garage yard where they had fixed my trailer lights. There was no one there, so I had to make a few phone calls to have someone come over and let me in. My Cherokee was finally hitched up to my trailer and ready to go. Canada here I come.

Six months later, the reckless driving charge was dropped. It cost me $1,600 in lawyer's fees. My defense was that I had consumed three large glasses of wine with my supper (over a period of two hours); and because I was on five different medications, I was seeing double and had sort of lost my senses. I was not charged with drunk driving or speeding, even though I had been driving very fast. Though the police officer knew this, I guess he figured that charging me with reckless driving was enough. It was just another bad sailing day. If I had been charged instead with one of the other two charges, I would have been allowed to bail myself out after my arraignment; and the bail would have been much less.

Back in Quebec, I sailed the *Kittiwake* for one season and then sold her to make room for another boat. I posted a For Sale sign on her bow, and 18 months later she was sold not before renovating her interior which was pathetic. I bought these boats because of their distinct looks and appeal. Each one had character and class. The wooden touch made the difference.

## Cornish Crabber / 2005

The *Cornish Crabber,* a gaff rigged cutter, fell into the same category as the other two boats, except that it had been made in England. The deck was twenty five feet long, and it was thirty feet length overall, with a five foot bowsprit and an eight foot beam. Its displacement was forty five hundred pounds, and it had a Yanmar diesel, 1-piston engine. The interior was very roomy. The mast, boom, and gaff were made of a spruce. The three sails were oxblood red, and the cabin roof was made of teak. The boat had a thirty inch draught keel up and a five foot draught keel down. The hull was forest green, and the deck was beige. It had a lazaret, propane, gimbaled, double burner, cooktop, and six brass portholes, which opened and closed. There were wooden slats on the floor as well as on the side bulkheads. I brought this little number home on her trailer. I thoroughly cleaned the interior and had all the interior cushions redone.

I planned to sail *Cornish Crabber* the next summer in 2010. The advantage of this boat was that I could haul it to the cottage and back home, saving myself winter marina fees; and this also permitted me to work on her at my home. The inside of the boat was very comfortable and homey. Another advantage was her shallow draught, which allowed me to come in close to shore; plus she wasn't too big to maintain. I was looking forward to sailing her. I installed a mooring in front of the cottage, which was on the Ottawa River next to the Lake of Two Mountains and I made a dock for her.

The crabbers sister ship in a full suit of sails.

The day of her purchase, there were better days in store for her.

# 21. The Heartbreaker

In 2005, with the boating season beginning, I had my eldest son, Francois, over to Oka Marina to do a tedious chore. We hoisted him up forty five feet into the air by a crane so he could make an adjustment to create a more precise parallel distance between *Mandolin Wind's* two masts. We had to spread them apart to the maximum that the turnbuckle would allow. This worked out just great. The masts were now perfectly parallel, as they should be. A paint touch-up on the hull and into the water she went for the new season. I installed all the necessary hardware and she was picture perfect. I had made a fore boom during the winter, and Frank (Francois) made the customized stainless parts to adapt to the boom. I installed a second staysail guy-wire from ¾ of the way up the mast and then (parallel to the genoa furler) running down to the second staysail deck fastener.

I purchased a used sail through *Boats for Sail* magazine and had it modified to fit the new boom as a boom staysail. When sailing, I would set a course with the mizzen set full sail, along with this boomed staysail, and the boat was in perfect balance. The helm held steady on its own. It was unbelievable. I had another sail cover made for this sail as well. Now the boat was fully dressed. She gave me a lot of enjoyment that year. I had a few ups and downs with her, but nevertheless, she was quite pleasant.

On one occasion, the boat made a 360-degree turn on itself as we were sailing, all on its own. I sort of guessed what had happened. A few seconds later, she did it again. My daughter told me to stop kidding around. I explained that I thought that the steering had gone afoul. We dropped anchor and sent out a radio call for help. "All stations, all stations." After a while, a small cruiser pulled up alongside to help us. He had heard our distress call. We tied her up parallel to the other boat, and slowly motored her back to her slip. Later, I found that the steering gear locking pin had broken.

On another occasion during a boat race, Frank and I were off to a very good start. Three quarters of the way through the race, I pushed her to her sailing limits and the steering gear broke this time. With my favorite engineer, Frank, we made a makeshift steering tiller to replace the wheel helm. This got us into port two hours later. The important thing we learned here was to get ourselves out of a hazardous maritime situation. A sailor must learn to rely on their own personal skills; there are no mechanics or tow trucks out on the water.

From that day on, it was smooth sailing except that there was more than one occasion where we had a hard time negotiating our way out of our slip. We had but 1½ boat lengths to maneuver backwards in, and there wasn't enough deep water beyond that point. The steering mechanism, when it had been manufactured, it was done in reverse (backwards or upside down), and this caused us increased headaches. We were always turning the wheel helm the wrong way when backing out. Once we even stayed stuck for a while. Our maneuvers looked very un-seamanlike, but we managed. Nonetheless, I savored every minute sailing, even the bad ones. My poor girlfriend, though, didn't like leaving the dock. We looked like a bunch of quacking ducks, all in disarray.

For those three years that *Mandolin Wind* was at the marina, she was berthed directly across from the *Osprey*. There was only a cement pier about 8 ft high that separated us. This was the service jetty. There were gas and diesel fuel and the pump-out at the end of this pier. What I liked was that I got to see my children often, even if it was only for a short talk. Sometimes Francois or Marc would come over, and we would have a beer and shared the week's news. We would talk of the progress we had made or that we would like to make on our own boats. Sometimes Roxanne would pop in, and we'd chat for a short while. There were times when we would have our favorite hotdogs under the canopy next to the pool or a full picnic meal together.

There was one embarrassing moment during the summer after my separation with Jacinthe. We had all gathered together for a late afternoon picnic after a day's sail on our two boats. There was Francois and Stephanie, Jacinthe and her sister Robin, Roxanne and her boyfriend, Marc and Marie Claude, and Florence and me. I was still suffering from this guilty and embarrassing complex about my separation with Jacinthe, being that it had been my fault. That was a long day in my life. It seemed that it would never end. On another day, I did take Jacinthe out on a sail, which was very pleasant. It was a promise I had made to her during our separation.

At Oka Marina, there was a big barbecue grill for everyone's use. Sometimes there could be as many as four or five families using it at the same time. It always worked out all right. There was always the kidding around or the friendly chat amongst us all. There were half a dozen picnic tables on the lawn as well as another six tables under the canopy. Eventually, there was a second barbeque unit installed.

There were toilets, showers, and vanities on the premises, which allowed us to shave and shower; plus we had a laundry room. There was a marina store nearby for hardware and boat supplies that you might need in an emergency and many practical items as well. I've always appreciated the owners of the Oka Marina, Marie and Claude. They have always been helpful when we were in need of something. I loved that place, maybe because they made me feel so at home.

The 2006 boating season started up without a snag. *Mandolin Wind* was at her berth. We went out on our weekend sails and picnics. Claude, the marina owner, asked me if I would re-varnish the woodwork on his forty two foot boat. The boat was a Gozard from the Bayfield family. This was the kind of boat that you just drooled over. He was going down south for the winter. I accepted the job. Here was a full-time job for a good part of the summer. I worked on his boat all week long, taking weekends off. During lunch hour, I would go and have lunch and coffee on my boat. Every day at 5 p.m., I would have a beer with Claude and then leave.

One Monday, a week before the construction holidays near the end of July, I was having lunch on board *Mandolin* when a question popped into my mind: how much water would come into the boat over a couple of days if the pump shut down? To answer this question, I shut off the bilge pump. The following day, I missed my chance to inspect the boat. The temperature outside had soared. With my heart condition, I couldn't put up with the heat; so I went home early. On Wednesday and Thursday, the same thing happened. Again on Friday morning, it was too hot; so I called Claude and told him that I would be back after my holidays in two weeks.

My girlfriend and I were going to spend our two-week vacation at our new cottage renovating. After the holidays, I didn't go to the marina on the Monday because of bad weather. The same thing happened on Tuesday. I did call Claude to make sure that he didn't worry and to let him know that I would be there once the foul weather was over. You can't varnish on rainy days or on hot, windy days.

That same Tuesday, it was blowing hard and raining all day. Around 7:00 p.m. I got a call from Claude that my boat was getting fairly full of water. I told him that I would be there in 40 minutes. Not even ten minutes later, the phone rang again. The boat had sunk at the dock. It was at the bottom. At this moment, it was as if I had lost a family member. I was in shock. I couldn't understand what had happened. There was nothing that we could do that night. He told me to bring in a big pump in the morning, one that had a four inch diameter evacuation line.

The following day, we phoned for a 100-ton crane to haul out the boat. That afternoon there was quite a stir at the marina. There were spectators everywhere. I felt foolish and hurt. One person asked me jokingly if my boat was part submarine. I laughed it off with a greenish grin. The crane operator drove out onto the pier right to the very end. With the harnesses in place, the crane started to lift the boat. When the boat's deck was lifted 1 ft above the water level, we started pumping. I dove underwater into the cabin and pulled out three beers. We saluted the crowd as we stood there having a beer for this special occasion. I was just trying to release my tension and accept what had happened.

When the boat was once again afloat, I noticed that the bilge pump switch was in the "Off" position. Then I remembered why! I didn't find out how much water the boat would take on in two days if the bilge pump was turned off; but I did find out that three weeks and three days was the time it took for my boat to take on enough water to sink! I think that might have been my very first sign of Alzheimer's.

The interior was smeared with motor oil, and all my cushions were soaked. Two months later, they still had not dried out. They ended up in the trash can, ($1000.00). The two batteries had exploded, so I had to buy new ones, ($300.00). I got a new GPS with a warranty, and I had my refrigerator fixed' ($180.00)… but not my heart. Crane operation cost and pump out machine, ($700.00). I'm sure I've forgotten some other expenses. I was so depressed that I never sailed her again. I worked hard to clean and wash away the oil that had soiled the inside of the boat. What a mess! A friend and I worked three days getting the motor running again. I spent the next three weeks trying to polish up the boat but it seemed like an endless chore. It was one thing after another. In the end, I motored around and that was about all. Inside, the flame had dwindled and died out. I was heartbroken.

September was here, and I had to finish Claude's boat. I had *Mandolin Wind* hauled out, and she stayed in dry dock for two sailing seasons. I had intended to repaint and re-varnish in the spring, but the passion was completely knocked out of me. I never found the courage to work on her again. I was not in shape to handle all the work again. I tried on three or four occasions, but my heart wasn't in it anymore. I still had this urge to sail *Mandolin Wind,* but my age got the best of me. Crazy as it may sound, but I felt as though I had lost my best friend. If I could have found another barn or garage, I could have refinished her; but I couldn't do it in the direct sunlight. The energy was all gone, sapped out of me. I let go of *Mandolin Wind.*

In the end, I sold the boat to a chap in December 2008. He was clearly excited about her. I was happy that there was someone to continue the saga. *Mandolin Wind* had another chance. He fell in love with her just as I had…

## Dying Is of Contemplation

Oh, wind so bold, so pounding cold,
Beating upon my chest,
Oh, thrusting waves, with all your craze,
Balance me upon each crest.

Frigid spray upon my face
That stings and tastes of salt,
A punishment I must embrace,
As though I were at fault.

With hands so numb and also sore,
My life is in my path,
I must fight back with ropes and chores,
When walking forw'rd and aft.

The seas are mean, I won't be seen,
If e'er I should fall in,
There's no one there, except despair,
And dying is of contemplation.

*Guy G. Lemieux*
*December, 1997*

# Epilogue

I worked on *Mandolin Wind* for seven years, 80 working days a year. I would recommend that you only do this if you like this kind of hobby. If not, it will become an endless chore that you will come to hate. It can be quite a challenge – keeping this as a hobby and because of your love for boats.

Sailing offers many benefits and pleasures. It's a water sport, a family sport, and it provides opportunities for daily and weekend outings. It's a cottage on water without the lawn cutting and taxes and house expenses such as telephone bills, because our cell phones will do the job. It's also a mode of transport. It's a place of gathering for family and friends. Sailing is a part of life. People can travel the world, and their children can get their education on board while traveling. There's always a way to fulfill our needs, our culture, our lives. In the warmer climates, some people live year after year on their boats and go to work in the city; and they still get to live their real, everyday life experiences and more.

One late September day, my girlfriend and I decided to go out for a sail. The sun was *"au rendezvous"* as we would say in French. Being it was a September day, the sun was there as if to greet us like a warm summer day. The air was silky soft, with an autumn perfume to it. We shoved off for the day with wine and cheese, crusty fresh bread, and grapes. There was barely a breeze; just enough that it tickled our cheeks as it slowly brushed by us. We decided to anchor in Parson's Bay.

Time was so subtle, so secretive. There was no noise and no movement, just the odd slap of water on the hull to remind us where we were, just the two of us. We brought out the wine and some food, along with a sleeping bag to make the deck softer. We laid it out on the foredeck just behind the bowsprit. My girlfriend sat with her back to the cabin front with her legs stretched out so as to capture the last tanning rays of the year. I had my camera with me, so I started to take a few pictures.

I wanted her to take off her top to sharpen up my boating pictures. She was reluctant to do so because of the houses along the shore. I answered her that there was no one on the lake and there was no one at the homes either, as it was a workday. I finally got to take a few pictures of her half-dressed, but in good taste, which she was proud of. I was just in love.

We felt totally free that afternoon. I'd have to say that it was the most beautiful day I have ever shared with someone. We didn't make love that afternoon; we didn't have to. Mother Nature did it for us. There were other instances that were very hot and comical as well, when we did make love. We had so many wonderful days sailing with our family and friends. We all enjoyed the experience.

Sometimes my girlfriend and I would go swimming bare bum, or in our birthday suits. At first my girlfriend was shy, but with time she came around. Francois, my gas boy (son), came to deliver some gas to me one day after I had run out. As he approached the boat, he saw that I was in my birthday suit and almost fell into the water. I wrapped a towel around my body. I felt like Popeye the sailor man. "Toot! Toot!"

Sometimes I did sight readings of the stars with Francois and Marc, or sometimes with my girlfriend. We would leave the marina in the middle of the night to get to a certain place in time to set the anchor and wait to take shots and readings. We would calculate our positions and compare them to the G.P.S. and the charts, and make comparisons with a handheld compass.

We also had memorable races. My daughter Roxanne competed in a number of races; mixed, single-handed, and all female. In one all-women's race in which she competed with a team, they won the race by winning back-to-back heats. The race was between four groups representing three marinas. She had learned a lot about this sport from two of her boyfriends. One was a sail maker by trade, and the other was an avid sailor. Francois raced a lot also with his brother or sister, or friends, or with me once in a while, and even with his girlfriend.

Francois and I were in this one race where we were sailing the *Osprey*, a Cal 25. We were in forth position and battling it out with a twenty five foot Tanzer on our transom. One of the three leaders ahead of us blew his spinnaker, and we picked up third place; but this Tanzer, named *Seahorse*, would not let up. To keep him at bay, we kept cutting across his bow, with me lying on the side of the hull as far as possible, hanging by one arm and one leg, to take his wind to give ourselves the slightest advantage. Would it be enough? It stayed this way to the very end, for 1 hour and 40 minutes. We finished in third by only a few seconds. We took one last tack, a bit too long, and they almost took advantage of that. We crossed the finish line just ahead of them by maybe one boat length. I wanted to place in this race very much for Francois.

I owed Francois this race for the other one we had lost. I'm sure he will remember it, as I do. You see, you cannot be two captains in charge of one boat. I couldn't keep still. I kept imposing my will on Francois, which caused conflicting decisions. I regretted that. He was the captain.

There were also hot and lazy days where we would drag one or two ropes behind the boat. Then one or two people would jump into the water and cool off, letting themselves get dragged by the ropes while under sail. Those were nice afternoons.

Today, Roxanne has her own sailboat, a 24-foot Mirage; and she sails it quite competently. She is a sailing instructor during the summer and gives basic navigation courses with the Canadian Power Squadron during the winter. The three kids sold the *Osprey,* the reason being that they were all heading for new horizons. The two boys will get back to the sport in due time; I'm almost sure of that. You see, they've bought a *Bombardier Invitation* just to toy with.

I did get to make love on the boat with the wildest and maddest passion a person could possibly have. I've felt all the joys that life could possibly bring. I never travelled far by boat, but I did get all the excitement that one could possibly have.

*One irony of this true story is that I had gone on a number of short trips with my dad to Port Dalhousie; and shortly after I had bought the* Mandolin Wind, *I found a sticker, well glued to one of its side portholes 43 years later. It bore the inscription:*

*"Port Dalhousie Yacht Club"*

*I never removed it. Was that a sign from you, Dad?*
*Thank you for guiding me towards our dreams.*

# Glossary

*afterdeck* (n.) the parts of the upper deck that lie to the rear of amidships

*beam* (n.) the width of a boat at her widest point

*bilge* (n.) the deepest part of a boat's hull (where any water that is leaking collects)

*binnacle* (n.) a stand used for a boat's compass that is placed near the helm

*boom* (n.) a horizontal pole used to wrap the foot of a sail onto to extend it

*boomkin* (n.) a short mizzen boom, used for extending a sail, securing blocks, and anchoring the sheets or the backstay from the mizzen

*boom vang* (n.) (martingale) a line or piston system, usually tackle- or lever-operated, used on a sailboat to exert downward pressure on the boom, so that the area of the mainsail facing the wind is maximized; usually extends from the boom to a location at the base of the mast

*boot stripe* (n.) a thin, straight line painted around the side of a boat that makes it look less bulky by making the boat look lower on the water

*bow* (n.) the forward part of a boat

*bowsprit* (n.) a short spar extending forward from the bow, normally used to anchor the forestay, to provide a wide bearing angle for support for the mast, and for rigging sails

*bulkhead* (n.) the vertical partition or wall on a boat that may be used to stiffen the hull and may be watertight; a retaining wall built along a waterfront

*bulwark* (n.) the sides of a boat that extend above the upper deck

*chine* (n.) a line that runs along the side of hull where the bottom joins the side, forming an angle (round bottom boats do not have this)

*cleat* (n.) a metal or wooden fixture having two horns around which ropes may be wrapped to make them secure

*crosstrees* (n.) two horizontal timbers mounted athwart ships (crosswise to the ship) at a masthead that are used to increase the angle of the shrouds (spread the shrouds out more) at the masthead in order to support the mast

*cutter* (n.) a single-masted, fore-and-aft rigged sailboat, in which the mast is just forward of the center line and carries several headsails

*deriveur* (n.) a small, shallow daysailer with a moveable keel

*doghouse* (n.) the part of the cabin that extends above the upper deck so as to provide more headroom

*doldrums* (n.) an area with a lack of wind; an area near the equator between the north and south trade winds having erratic light winds; and area between the trade winds and the Westerlies that has a lack of wind and heavy swells

*draft* (n.) the vertical distance from a boat's waterline and the deepest part of the keel; the vertical distance (from a boat's waterline downward) of water a boat will draw

*empennage* (n.) a jibe; a change of direction with the wind at your back

*espars* (n.) a pole used to raise the top of a sail, as on schooners; a gaff *fender* (n.) a cushion (as a tire, rope, foam rubber strip, or wooden float) that is attached to the side of a boat to lessen shock and prevent damage

*fetch* (n.) the distance over which wind blows or waves run unobstructed before it reaches a certain point

*foc* (n.) a jib; a small, forward sail

*fo'c'sle, forecastle* (n.) the compartment on a sailboat that is most forward; a compartment forward of the mast where the seamen's berths are located

*foot straps* (n.) the straps into which a sailor can put their feet to steady themselves if a boat lists too much, or to keep the boat in balance by leaning out from the boat opposite the direction of the heeling

*fore boom* (n.) the boom that stretches the foresail to an open position

*foredeck* (n.) the part of a boat's main deck that is near the bow

*forepeak* (n.) the forward most compartment in the bow of a boat, often used for storing the anchor rode or sails

*freeboard* (n.) the distance between the upper deck and the waterline or between the gunwale and the waterline

*gaff* (n.) a spar that the head of a fore-and-aft sail is stretched out on; long pole used to push off the dock with or to bring a boat close to the dock

*genoa* (n.) a large foresail that overlaps the mainsail and offers great power

*gooseneck* (n.) a fitting at the forward end of the boom that connects the boom to the mast

*grab rail* (n.) a sturdy railing that is installed along passageways for people to grab hold of while moving about a boat

*gunwale* (n.) the uppermost edge of the side of a boat (from the place where one would rest a gun)

*guy* (n.) a line used to control the end of a spar, such as when a spinnaker pole has one end attached to the mast, while the free end is moved back and forth using a guy

*guy-wire, guy-rope* (n.) a cable designed to add stability to a structure, such as a boat's mast

*halyard* (n.) an arrangement of lines and blocks to hoist a sail or flag

*hank* (n.) snap hooks, rings, or clips sewn to the luff of a sail or jib and used to attach it to the stay

*hatch* (n.) an opening in the cabin or the deck of a boat that gives access below; cover for such an opening

*head* (n.) a toilet compartment; a toilet

*headsail* (n.) any sail mounted forward of the forward most mast

*heel* (v.) to lean or tip to one side because of the force of the wind on the sails; to cause to lean or tip to one side

*helm* (n.) a wheel, tiller, or lever used to steer a boat

*hitch* (n.) a knot; a bend made in a rope to secure it to a fitting

*jib* (n.) a triangular headsail mounted on a stay that extends from the foremast head to the bowsprit or jibboom a small forward sail

*jibe* (v.) to change tacks when sailing with the wind by steering away from the wind so that the leech of the sail swings across the eye of the wind and the boom transfers from one side of the boat to the other

*jibboom* [*jib-boom, jib boom*] (n.) the removable spar that extends from the bowsprit that is used for mounting a flying jib

*keel* (n.) the backbone of a boat; the main longitudinal structural member of a boat to which all the frames, ribs, and other main structural supports are fastened

*ketch* (n.) a two-masted, fore-and-aft rigged sailboat with the mainmast mounted forward of the beam, and a mizzenmast mounted forward of the mainmast *lazaret* (n.) a stowage compartment located below the afterdeck (toward the stern)

*lee cloth* (n.) a cloth, also referred to as a Bunk Guard, installed on the open side of a bunk to stop someone who is sleeping from falling out of the bunk in severe conditions

*leech, leach* (n.) the vertical edge of a sail

*lifelines* (n.) fencing made of wire, or a rope, etc., and stanchions, installed around the edge of a boat to prevent people from falling overboard

*list* (v.) to lean to one side, usually because of unbalanced weight or damage to the hull

*luff* (n.) the forward edge of a fore-and-aft sail

*mainmast* (n.) the main and highest mast on a sailboat

*mainsail* (n.) the main and largest sail on a sailboat

*mainsheet* (n.) the tackle used to secure and control the angle of the mainsail to the wind

*mast* (n.) a vertical pole used to support sails, booms, shrouds, etc.

*mizzen* (n.) a fore-and-aft sail flown on the mizzenmast

*mizzenmast* (n.) the smaller aftermost mast on a sailboat

*planks* (n.) strakes; the longitudinal boards forming the hull of a wooden boat

*port* (n.) the left side of a vessel as seen by someone facing the bow; from the ancient use of an oar or steering board that was installed on the starboard side, making it necessary to approach a dock, or port, on the port (left) side

*pulpit* (n.) a secure railing on the bowsprit that extends over the bow and provides a lookout position, a place to tend sails, or a place to attach lifelines

*pump-out services* (n.) services provided for the pumping out of sewage on a boat

*rail* (n.) a sturdy barricade installed at the edge of the deck for the safety for passengers and crewmembers

*reef* (v.) to reduce the area of a sail during rough winds by rolling, folding, or securing the lower part at reef points

*rode* (n.) a rope or chain used to secure the anchor to the boat

*roller furler* (n.) a system for managing a sail's size by rolling it on a rotating stay to reduce or increase its size

*roller reefer* (n.) a system for managing a sail's size by rolling it on a rotating boom to reduce or increase its size

*rub-rail, rubrail* (n.) a board attached along the rail or along the hull that runs the length of the boat that protects the hull when the boat is alongside a dock or other boat

*rudder* (n.) a plate or blade positioned underwater at the stern, controlled by the helm or rudder handle to steer the boat

*schooner* (n.) a boat having two or more masts bearing fore-and-aft sails, with the mizzen forward of the mainmast

*sheet* (n.) a sail, or a line used to control the angle of a sail

*sheet block* (n.) a block and tackle system used to control the angle of the mainsail

*shroud* (n.) a lateral support, usually made of wire, metal cable, or metal rod, for the mast

*slip* (n.) an area between two piers for docking a boat

*sloop* (n.) a sailboat having a single mast mounted forward of the beam and a single jib

*spinnaker* (n.) a large, triangular sail, flown in front of all other sails, used for sailing downwind *stanchion* (n.) an upright post, bar, or support installed on the edge of the upper deck (as for support for a roof or for attaching cables or a rail to for gripping for safety)

*starboard* (n.) the right side of a vessel as seen by someone facing the bow

*stay* (n.) a thick rope or metal cable used to support a mast fore and aft

*staysail* (n.) a triangular fore-and-aft sail that is set on a stay with hanks

*stem* (n.) the forward most upright structural member at the bow, referring to the timber between the forward end of the keel and the deck

*stern* (n.) the rear most part of the hull, referring to the part between the rear end of the keel and the deck

*sternpost* (n.) main member of the stern, which extends from the keel to the deck

*tack* (n.) the direction of a sailboat; the length travelled on one tack; a tight turn from starboard to port or vice versa

*starboard tack* (n.) sailing with the wind coming from the starboard side of the vessel; on a starboard tack

*port tack* (n.) sailing with the wind coming from the port side of the vessel; on a port tack

*tack* (v.) to make a tight turn from starboard to port or vice versa

*tiller* (n.) a long, rigid lever attached to the top of the rudder, used to steer a vessel

*toe-rail, toe rail, toe rail* (n.) a bulwark; a low partition around the edge of a sailboat, sometimes slotted to allow drainage

*topsail, tops'l* (n.) any loose-footed sail set above the other sails on a mast

*topside* (adv.) on the deck

*topsides* (adv.) part of the hull above the waterline

*transom* (n.) the flat surface at the stern of the hull (running from keel to deck)

*trunk* (n.) a large structure built above the deck to allow headroom below; the part of the cabin extending above deck; housing for a rudder or centerboard

*turnbuckle* (n.) a mechanism consisting of a link threaded like a screw at the two ends, which connects to a shroud or stay and is turned to bring the two ends closer together and put more tension on the shroud or stay

*v-berth* (n.) the berth in the bow area

*wheel* (n.) a wheel, usually with spokes, by which a helmsman steers the vessel; the propeller

*windlass* (n.) a winch powered by electricity or steam with a shaft and two drums for raising a vessel's anchor

*yawl* (n.) a two-masted sailboat with the mainmast set forward of the beam and the mizzenmast set far aft

# About the Author

A machinist, cabinet maker and a draughtsman, along with many other qualities such as an entrepreneur and sales were my resources'. Reading is a contributing factor and I had the gift to read both in English and French, therefore my access was wide open to reading materials. True stories from England, France, and the United States, all this on sailing and boats, naturally.

I learned firsthand on how to sail a sailboat. I learned to repair, renovate and build and remodel wooden boats. Talent was probably part of me and skill came with time.

I lived the first 26 years in Ontario near Niagara Falls and the last 40 years in Québec near Montréal. I was always dreaming and fantasizing with every project that I did. It gave me that challenge and drive, to try to excel. Whether it was in leadership, golf, swimming and sailing.